Village Profiles

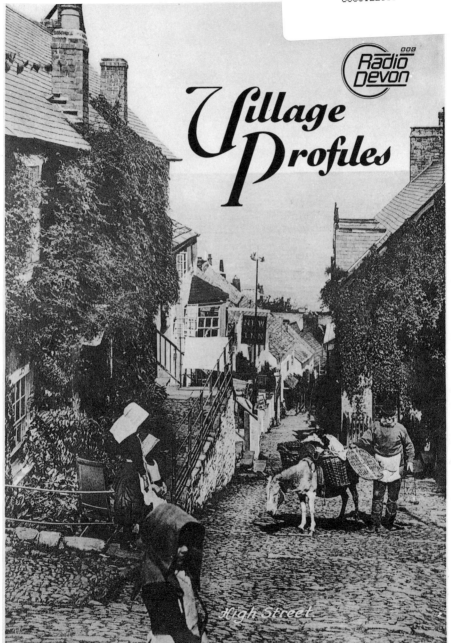

High Street

1

Up

Village Profiles

A personal view
of some of Devon's villages
based on the
BBC Radio Devon Series,
presented and written by
CHRIS SMITH

Original line drawings
by
ROBIN MURRAY

Published by QUAY BOOKS Exeter, The Quay, Exeter, DEVON.

First published 1990. All rights reserved.

Copyright BBC Radio Devon, Chris Smith and Robin Murray.

Photographs as credited. 1990.

To Lucy, Ben and Flora with love. This one's for you. In memory of those
long hours away from home on the Village Profile trail, to all those I
met and with thanks for the wonderful hospitality provided on the way.

Foreword
by Rolf Harris

Dear Chris —

What a long time ago it all was... I was
courting my wife and we have just celebrated our
32nd wedding anniversary. We had gone to Chagford
to stay with her parents and although my memories
of those days are vague, I know that the weather was
beautiful as my wife to be scolded me for talking
too much as we lay on our backs soaking up the sun.

She kept saying " Shh.... just listen!" and
I can still conjure up the abiding memory of the
warmth of the sun and the buzz of the bees going
about their business.

I certainly don't recall meeting the
young Chris Smith but I can imagine that it may
have made an impression on him because I was on
TELEVISION!! Television itself seemed to be a very
new thing. The commercial channel had just come into
being and rightly, or wrongly, it had an air of
being the rebel as opposed to the staid and established
BBC.

I was, I think, the only person to be
working regularly on both the BBC and Redifusion
where I told stories about Oliver the Octopus which
I drew on paper and also brought to life by drawing
on my hand, something that obviously Chris remembers
and I wish that I recalled more but I was I think
more concerned with making friends with my beloved's
standard poodle "Puggsy" who was very jealous of me
and made it obvious by turning her back on me whenever
I appeared.

6

Anyway Chris, to make amends, here's a picture of
Oliver in both his forms and may I wish you all
kinds of success with this book.

I assure you that I wasn't the cause of the
"Beverley" closing down as a guest house and I wish
it were possible to go back now to the Beverley as
it was then in those quieter, calmer days.

Cheers

Introduction

It all started with a newspaper advert, although I cannot remember the exact wording. It read something like 'New BBC Radio Station, opening in January, looking for Breakfast Show Presenter.' Just up my street I thought. After all I had worked for the BBC (Television) in the early seventies and it was all part of the same family so to speak, the job was almost mine...

Having read on, I realised, to my horror, the advert asked would be applicants to submit a 'demo tape', although at that stage the relevance of such a request escaped me,which was as good an indication of how green I was in terms of radio and broadcasting as any. However I could learn and I knew that an old friend of mine was working as a Programme Controllor of an Independent Radio Station in Middlesborough and that he would help out in 'my hour of need'. A telephone call later the friend had suggested that I head north, having recorded 'a couple of interviews on reel to reel' (whatever that meant) and he would help me put together the required demo in the radio station studios. Ironically the old friend, Dave Cousins, now runs the Independent Radio station in Exeter based only a few hundred yards from the doors to Radio Devon's studios.

After having interviewed a highly suspicious pig farmer about his computerised breeding system and a local man who farms with heavy horses and who subsequently became a friend of mine I set off for my first excursion into the realm of broadcasting and climbed aboard a coach for Yorkshire to make my tape and, I hoped, ultimately my fortune.

I still have that tape and inspite of my friend's production and the skills of the local radio engineer, to this day I remember with awe the way that he edited the tape that we did and made the whole thing hang together, my demo fell on 'deaf ears·' at the BBC and didn't land me the coveted Breakfast Show Presenter's job. Having listened to the tape again recently I cannot really say that I am surprised. I sound stilted, very un-natural and fell right into the beginners' trap of 'Broadcasting' ie shouting to the world, little realising that the skill lies in being able to talk as one would in everyday conversation as if you are just talking to one person and not as if you were addressing a large political rally!!

Looking back I suppose that I am grateful that things turned out as they did because the prospect of getting up at four in the morning to go on air at six fills me with horror. It's not so much the time of day because I had spent seven years market gardening and early rising didn't worry me, it's the prospect of having to be happy, bright and breezy 'live on air' at that time of the day that would worry me – a patch of cabbage or sprouts couldn't care less if your mood be fair or foul, a radio audience could, and undoubtedly would.At the time however I have to confess to more than a tinge of disappointment when the then Programme Organiser of BBC Radio Devon, Mike Gibbons, wrote back, my having inflicted him with the demo tape, saying that he felt that my presentation style was not quite right for their breakfast programme but that if I had any ideas for 'feature' type material then do please get in touch again.

Whether or not this was really the polite 'brush off', his version of the 'thanks for your interest, but no thanks' type of letter I'm not sure, but having 'recovered' from not being rocketed to radio stardom as a presenter I quickly responded to Mike's letter with a 'feature' idea that I have to confess was not entirely original as those listeners to Radio Four will appreciate. I'm sure that Mike Gibbons too appreciated that the idea had been tried and tested elsewhere than on Radio Devon, when I wrote to him suggesting a Village Profile type 'Down Your Way' programme idea. After a short silence from the Radio Devon end, I then received a letter from Mike Gibbons inviting me to go into the offices to meet with him and discuss the idea further.

I remember explaining to this great huge man with a ginger beard who looked more like a whaling captain than a broadcaster (whatever broadcasters look like) with what I hoped was great flair and originality that the idea was to go to a different Devon Village every week, fortnight or whatever and paint a thumb nail sketch, through the words of those that lived there, of life in that particular place – A Village Profile.

To my great surprise and I suppose at the time enormous relief he liked the idea, 'commissioned' me to start on a series of 'profiles' under the watchful eye, ears and guiding hand of an experienced Radio Four Producer, Irene Mallis, who had joined Radio Devon to launch the station 'on air.'

Over the next few months I rapidly learned the basics of radio and probably made all the mistakes in the book but with Irene's infinite patience, and I have to say trust, I think that I turned in some reasonable radio. This was really little to do with me but much to do with the people who were kind enough to talk to me when I arrived in their village or community armed with the trusty tape recorder and clutching a handful of BBC Radio Devon leaflets.I was greatly assisted and supported in the early days by the Community Council of Devon, James Derounian and Dennis Reed in particular, who suggested places to visit and who I should contact and over the years I travelled the length and breath of the county, clocking up thousands of miles on the Village profile trail. The result was over a hundred broadcast programmes, all archived in the Radio Devon library, many many hours of work and travel in all weathers, the enormous pleasure in meeting so many wonderful people who received me so warmly and now this book which was born out of the experience of producing and presenting BBC Radio Devon's Village Profiles series. It is not intended as a guide book nor a rose coloured spectacled look at life in some thirty of Devon's villages selected for this collection but rather a personal record of how it seemed to me and how people told me their story at the time... Many of the people I spoke with during the course of the series are no longer with us, but their voices are captured forever in the BBC Radio Devon Sound Library, so too is the spirit of these, just some of Devon's villages, contained in this collection of BBC Radio Devon Village Profiles.

BBC RADIO DEVON
PO BOX 5
CATHERINE STREET
PLYMOUTH PL1 2AD
TELEPHONE: 0752 260323
FAX: 0752 222679

Village Profile was a highly successful series which was broadcast by BBC Radio Devon on a regular basis for five years. The concept was not new. It was really a local version of "Down Your Way", but there is no doubt that it helped establish a strong rapport between the radio station and its audience. It also helped listeners throughout the county to learn more about themselves and their neighbours. On many occasions, there were reminders about how life used to be in years gone by, and some marvellous characters - and associated yarns - were uncovered.

Those programmes now serve as a permanent audio archive of life in many of our Devon villages. It is an archive we are proud to accommodate; and indeed it is still expanding with the "Our Place" features each weekday. Village Profile brought pleasure to hundreds of listeners; I hope you enjoy reading this book as much as listening to the series.

ROY CORLETT
Manager

FM STEREO PLYMOUTH 103.4MHZ   EXETER 95.8MHZ   NORTH DEVON 94.8MHZ   OKEHAMPTON 96.0MHZ
AM PLYMOUTH 855KHZ/351M   EXETER 990KHZ/303M   NORTH DEVON 801KHZ/375M   TORBAY 1458KHZ/206M

Index

Aylesbeare

Like many people, long before I became involved with BBC Radio
Devon and the Village Profile series, I had first heard of the small
East Devon village of Aylesbeare in 1978. It was in the late summer
of that year that the name and that of the missing village school girl,
Genette Tate, became headline news.

On the afternoon of Saturday August 19th, thirteen year old
Genette completely disappeared during her afternoon newspaper
delivery round and as a result one of the biggest police hunts ever
was mounted in Devon. Genette was last seen by two of her friends
in Within Road, only half a mile out of the centre of the village. Just
ten minutes later her bicycle was found by the friends, laying on its
side with the newspapers scattered on the road around it.

At first the friends thought that Genette was playing some kind of
practical joke on them and was hiding somewhere, but a search of
the adjacent fields and hedgerows by her friends revealed nothing.
Nor did a search by their parents. The·alarm was raised and the
police called in. All available officers were drafted into the area, a

R.A.F. helicopter was called to assist and the massive hunt for the missing schoolgirl was underway.

The Aylesbeare village hall became an incident control centre and over the next few weeks more than eighty police, helped by people from the village and the local area, combed the countryside for a five mile radius around the village. The Royal Marines were called in from nearby Lympstone to help and on one Sunday afternoon more than 7,000 members of the public joined in a search of Woodbury Common; even the then Chief Constable, John Alderson, joined the search parties.

The search for Genette led by Chief Constable John Alderson.

In spite of intensive efforts and media attention – there can hardly have been anyone in the country who didn't know that Genette had seemingly vanished from the face of the earth or know what she looked like – no trace of the girl was found. Additional helicopters joined the hunt, aircraft criss-crossed the Devon landscape equipped with the latest in photographic equipment, mounted police and police dogs joined in, police divers searched streams, rivers and gravel pits but no clue was unearthed as to what had happened to the girl. She had quite simply disappeared. In the space of ten minutes Genette Tate had gone and all that remained was her bike. The only possible 'lead' that the police had was the description of a car which had been seen travelling towards the village at about the time she disappeared, but this didn't help too much. The witness couldn't say what the registration number was and couldn't be certain whether the car had been brown or red and no driver ever came forward so the car remains as much of a mystery to this day as does Genette's disappearance. It's one Devon and Cornwall Police file that isn't closed.

It was some five years after Genette's disappearance that I went to Aylesbeare to record the Village Profile programme. My first impression was of the wide mix and variety of buildings and I was also struck by the fact that there's a working farm right in the village centre. The place has grown enormously over the centuries, although surprisingly less than five hundred people live in the village now. But Stanley Turl can remember when there were only twenty houses – "The council house building started in 1931 with just four houses and since then another twenty six council houses have gone up and another twenty or so private ones."

Like so many Devon villages, Aylesbeare used to be populated by farmers, farm labourers and people who earned their living off the land. Things have changed a great deal with most people having to travel out of the village to find work. With busy Exeter Airport, still expanding, right on the doorstep, some find employment there, others commute to Exeter itself and there are a handfull of small businesses in the village itself. One of these is the Aylesbeare Post Office which Lyn Stansell set up in her garage!

"There used to be a Post Office here, but about five years ago the Post Master wanted to retire but didn't want to move out from where he was living, which was the Post Office. We were anxious that the village shouldn't lose its Post Office and so I volunteered for the job."

Lyn had to get formal approval by the Post Office authorities and having done this, it was then a question of finding the premises. Enter Lyn's husband, Martin, who luckily is a builder by trade. He set about converting their garage into a Post Office and Shop and today their 'garage' has become not only a place to buy stamps but a meeting place for villagers where they can have a chat, and even a cup of tea.

Aylesbeare is a very close knit community which is perhaps one of the reasons why Genette's disappearance shook the village to its very roots. Today it is patrolled by a warden system as Gerald Binmore explained – "The village is split into areas and each area has its own warden. They keep an eye on those in their patch" in case of illness or need – "and also supply them with a copy of Aylesbeare Topics" a sort of cross between a Parish Magazine and a newspaper.

Ivy Timms is the editor and she has seen the paper grow from a single foolscap sheet to a twenty page booklet. "We have everything we can in the paper" she said "from stories and jokes to adverts and news." One of the more unusual ads that caught my eye was the twice yearly visit of the blood donors van. This is largely the brainchild of 'Timmy's' husband, Arthur. He originally contacted the Blood Transfusion Service and was told that if he could guarantee 120 or more donors on a visit then it would be worth their while coming to Aylesbeare. Arthur set about 'recruiting' donors, found more than the required number and now twice a year the village donates blood. I can't think of any other village in the county who run their own blood bank.

Aylesbeare has of course survived the disappearance of Genette Tate, although it left deep scars which haven't healed to this day. When I was there, few would talk about those days or what they thought had happened to her. But for all that, it's a thriving little community which supports its own school, village hall, a church, chapel and pub. Nick Pratt, a young man in his twenties, summed it up really – "It may not be the most exciting place, but it's not really quiet either. It's just a nice place to live. I love it."

Bickleigh

What's the connection between Paul Simon, the singer, the Chardonnay grape, the headless horseman and the oldest building in Devon? If that sounds like a question from BBC Television's 'Mastermind' on which you would have to pass, then the answer is in fact quite easy and you'd have to look no further than the village of Bickleigh near Exeter.

Situated in the Exe valley on the route to Tiverton, the road takes you over a bridge which in places is so narrow it only allows for single file traffic. On the far bank you will find two of Devon's most famous pubs, the Fisherman's Cott and the more picturesque Trout Inn. It is one of these pubs that provides the clue to Paul Simon's link with Bickleigh as it is reputed that whilst staying at the Fisherman's Cott, he was inspired by Bickleigh's bridge over the wide, fast flowing River Exe, to compose his classic song 'Bridge Over Troubled Waters.'

Paul Simon, writer of Bridge Over Troubled Waters.

High above Bickleigh you will find the Chardonnay grape grown in Yearlstone Vineyard from which Gillian Pearkes produces some excellent English table wines.

It is on Bickleigh's Bridge that you may see the Headless Horseman ride by on Mid-Summer Night's Eve and the oldest building is to be found at Bickleigh's very own castle.

Before you come to the bridge, travelling from the Exeter direction, set back from the road is Bickleigh Mill which when I visited the village was owned and run by Bill Shields. It had opened as a tourist attraction in 1973 and beside the enormous working water wheel, a wonderful sound background on radio, Bill had told me of how the place had developed from a working mill to a farm centre where visitors could see traditional craftspeople at work, cows being milked by hand, farm machinery that has long since disappeared and some of the less common breeds of farm animal, as well as being able to go trout fishing in the nearby ponds. The Mill also provided a limited amount of local employment and although I haven't been there for several years now, it provided a lot of pleasure for my young family when we last visited.

It was in the village centre, at Lilac Cottage, that Arthur Buttle, a long time resident, told me of the story of Bickleigh's ghost. "One Midsummer's Eve, one of the Carew family was courting Elizabeth Courtney from Bickleigh Castle, near the bridge.One of the Cruwys from Cruwys Morchard came down to the bridge, which was a wooden bridge then, and started a fight over the girl. The Cruwys killed the Carew and horse and rider went in over the bridge and crashed down into the river. Both were killed by drowning, if not by the sword. It's said that at midnight on Midsummer Night's Eve you can see the figure of a horseman on the bridge carrying his head under his arm. I've never been down there to see if it's true, but the man that killed him was granted a pardon on condition that his family gave up thirteen manors of land to the Carews and that is how the Carew family came into possession of the parish." It's a story that I have never put to the test, but perhaps one Midsummer's Eve I will mount a vigil on Bickleigh's Bridge over Troubled Waters,having fortified myself first at one of the two pubs!

If you are able to cross the bridge without hinderance from the Headless Horseman or the modern day articulated truck, you turn off to Bickleigh Castle, now the home of Noel and Norma Boxall. It stands on the site of an early Norman Castle which was destroyed by Cromwell, replaced by a fortified manor house which too was destroyed but from which remains what is said to be the oldest complete building in Devon, the old Chapel, which stands over the road from the castle itself. I can vividly remember Norma taking me into the chapel and unlocking the doors with the biggest key I have ever seen. Many houses like Bickleigh Castle have passed into the hands of the National Trust for 'safe keeping' largely because of the enormous expense of upkeep and repair, but not so Bickleigh Castle. Still privately owned and lived in by the Boxalls it's open from Easter to the Autumn and is really beautifully kept and in excellent condition thanks to their dedication and hard work. One surprising aspect of a visit there was the exhibition of artefacts from the Mary Rose, King Henry Vlll's warship. I was fascinated by this having been glued to my television set when the ship was lifted off the seabed under the watchful eye of the Prince of Wales. It was a triumph of modern technology and engineering and I have promised myself one day a visit to the hull which is in Portsmouth, and is constantly sprayed with salt water to help preserve it.

Noel Boxall explained that when the Mary Rose sank, the Admiral in charge of her and the fleet had been Sir George Carew, an ancestor of the Bickleigh Bridge 'horseman', who had lived at the Castle as a child. It seems that the Carews were cursed by water and Sir George Carew drowned when the Mary Rose went down in 1545, but to this day the memory of him and his ship live on in Bickleigh.

My visit to the village ended with a visit to Bickleigh's very own vineyard run by Gillian Pearkes on a hillside overlooking the river valley. It was early in the year and she had just completed her meticulous pruning of the vines laid out in long, straight ranks running north to south. There is a lot of confusion over what an English wine is, as opposed to British wines which seem to be flooding the market recently. A British wine is something that is produced from blending grape juices from various countries to produce a sort of hybrid product not truely having any real nationality. An English wine, however, is made from crushing grapes which are grown in this country. Gillian produces English wines which to my inexperienced palate are of a superb quality. English wine has perhaps an undeservedly bad reputation, largely due I suspect to confusion over exactly what an English wine is but Gillian's Madeline Angevine and her Chardonnay rank more than favourably with 'quality' French or German vintages. I was surprised, although I don't really know why I should have been, as climatically in the warm environs of the South West we often differ little from the wine producing regions of the Continent in terms of sunshine and temperature, although looking back over some of our recent summers perhaps that is difficult to appreciate. What is certain is that Gillian's wine has to be tasted to be truely appreciated and a mark of its quality is that it has found its way onto tables, not only locally in Bickleigh and Devon but far beyond the county borders in smart London restaurants. Altogether Bickleigh is a most surprising place and even if you never go there you will now be much better placed should you ever find yourself on 'Mastermind', faced with the question I posed at the beginning of this Village Profile. And every time I hear that Paul Simon song performed by him and his partner Art Garfunkel, I am reminded of the tiny Devon village of Bickleigh.

Blackawton

The Village Profile of Blackawton started with the American National Anthem, 'The Stars and Stripes' and a voice over reading these words – "This memorial was presented by the United States Army Authorities to the people of the South Hams who generously left their homes and lands to provide a battle practice area for the succesful assault on Normandy in June 1944. Their action resulted in the saving of many hundreds of lives and contributed in no small measure to the success of the operation. The area included the villages of Blackawton, Chillington, Slapton..."

It is difficult today, nearly fifty years after the event, to appreciate the impact that this 'Dress Rehearsal' by the Americans for the invasion of Europe must have had on the tranquil peace of this corner of Devon. It's often said that memory is short and that scars heal quickly but there are many still in the area who remember well how the war came to Blackawton and its consequences.

Blackawton is one of the largest parishes in the South Hams, with rolling countryside, deep valleys and lush green hills, prime dairy farming country.High banked lanes bordering narrow lanes dissect the area which is well served by three pubs, village stores, Post Office and a bakery. The bakery was my first point of call where the Edmonds family have been baking bread for the parish since 1954. Their working day starts at half past three in the morning, long before even the farmers have climbed wearily from their beds. When they first started as village bakers Arthur Edmonds told me that they "Used to weigh everything by hand and mix the dough by hand as well. Now days it's all done by machine and we bake somewhere around three hundred loaves a day. Most of it we deliver. Years ago the ovens used to be coke fired but we changed over to oil and that's how we do it today."

Not much of the old ways of doing things have survived in working the bakery aside from the loaf tins, some of which date back to 1948 and are still used today.

In 1948, the village must have only just returned to 'normal' following the arrival and departure for the beaches of France by the American troops who had been stationed in the area. Alan Buckpit, whose family have lived in the parish for over two hundred years, recalled those times for me. "In 1943, my sister was out selling poppies round about the end of the first week of November. She came home and told us that she had heard rumours that the Blackawton area and other villages were going to be evacuated for training for the American troops. I said that it was most ridiculous and impossible and that it would never happen. But within a few days there was notices placed around the village calling us to a meeting in the church. There they told us exactly what was going to happen."

"The Americans were just beginning to get into the area and at that time the news media was censored and we knew very little about what was going on, even from one village to the next. At the church meeting we were told that the area was required for Americans and English soldiers to practice for a landing that was to be made across the channel in the foreseeable future and that we just had to go, and go we did. My family was fortunate in that part of our farm was in the area to be evacuated and part was out and we moved into a vacant bungalow on the boundaries of the farm."

I asked Alan what he could remember of the events that followed? "We saw quite a lot of Americans, we'd meet them when they came and parked up beside the road. You'd chat with them but you never really got to know exactly who they were or where they came from. They didn't really want to be here but they, like us, were in the war to win it. They were just ordinary people from all walks of life and we found them very friendly. We didn't really see much of what was going on, but we heard the gun fire from the ships out at sea firing over the troops as they landed on the beaches. As boys we used to go into the restricted area, which was very silly really and we'd meet some of the Americans and they would be as scared as we were."

During the rehearsals lives were actually lost, an indication of how 'real' the manoeuvres were and Alan told me that at the time although the villagers had known that some men had died they didn't really appreciate the extent of what had happened. "It was rumoured that large numbers had been killed but we never knew for sure."

Speculation on what happened in those far off days has increased over the years, with some claiming that hundreds died when one particular excercise went disastrously wrong, there are even those who think that the fields around the village are the final resting place for some of the Americans who died, some being buried on Alan's farm.

"That's the biggest load of rubbish I've ever heard" he said. "I walked those fields where the Americans are supposedly buried every day during the war and not one turf was moved in that field. They may have been given temporary burial in the area but the Americans, like our service people, looked after their dead and respected them and I'm sure that after the war they were taken to wherever for a decent burial."

Nevertheless the rumours still abound to this day of the D-Day landing rehearsal that went wrong, of hundreds who died and were left buried, forgotten heroes in the fields of South Devon. Perhaps we will never know for sure what happened although what is certain is that at nearby Slapton stands a memorial to the people of Blackawton and the area, who sacrificed their homes during this period, and it's captured in Leslie Thomas's novel 'The Magic Army'.

After hearing Alan's recollection of the war coming to Blackawton, I felt in need of some liquid refreshment and headed out of the village to Blackawton Brewery where Nigel Fitzhugh, who founded the business, allowed me to taste a pint of Blackawton Bitter whilst telling me about the brewing process. "I was living in the village,

Nigel Fitzhugh working in Blackawton Brewery.

doing something else and thought that I needed to change my means of income and thought what can I do? I was a home brewer, just like a lot of other people are, and I thought that it would be a rather novel idea to start brewing beer commercially and sell it. So I turned my hobby into a commercial business and it went off like a rocket from the start."

To brew beer you simply need yeast, malt, hops and water and this is all that Nigel uses to produce his beers in an enormous barn set away from the house where he and his family live. The result is a traditional 'real' ale. The malt comes from the last maltster in the South West based in Newton Abbot who produces malt from the barley grown locally in Devon. Initially the malt is crushed, steeped in hot water, then mashed for a few hours for the sugar to be extracted from the malt giving a liquid wort mixture which runs into a copper boiler where it is brought to the boil and hops added. This gives the beer the bitter taste and the traditional 'brewery' smell is produced. The liquid is then cooled and passes into a fermenting vessel where the yeast is added at a particular temperature. Some four days later after the yeast has 'eaten' up the sugar, the liquid converts into alcohol. I wondered at what stage Nigel put his taste buds to work. "I can tell more what's going on by smell, at the various different stages of brewing. I don't taste it until after the fermentation stage. Then it goes into casks, with finings, which make the yeast drop out of the beer allowing the publican to draw off a clear pint from the barrel".

When Nigel started in 1977, he was one of the first to produce real ale which gave him a head start in marketing and for the first two or three years had little difficulty in selling what he brewed. "Life now, however, is not as easy as it was because the big boys, the large breweries, saw that there was a demand for real ale and they jumped on the bandwagon. Today I've got some sixty five customers, most of which are pubs, so things are going alright."

I sampled a pint of Nigel's bitter, toasted his health and drank to the continued success of Blackawton Brewery having enjoyed my visit to a village that remembered vividly the day that the Second World War came to Devon.

Branscombe

Branscombe, on the East Devon coast, has a special place in this book and is also a place that I vividly remember visiting as it was the first village in the series that the Producer sent me to and in many ways it proved a difficult place to follow ... however, we managed. Subsequently I returned there and did a longer version of the original programme which formed the first ever Village Profile that Radio Devon broadcast. I also remember, as if it were only yesterday, the real thrill my wife and I got when the (then) presenter of the morning programme 'cued' in the start of that Branscombe Village Profile and the series was 'on the air', as we listened at home in the kitchen.

Within its long meandering main street, which eventually leads to the pebbled beach, when I first went to Branscombe, within yards of each other, you could find Devon's only working woman blacksmith in her forge opposite the wood fired village bakery and, in the square, the village stores run by the Bakers' sister, Ivy Collier.

The National Trust, who own and safeguard much of the local coastline here, also own the bakery which has been closed for several years and is now a tea room and museum. The Trust also own the thatched forge which is rented by Lyn Bagwell and her husband who work there with the furnace roaring, beating red hot metal into ornate iron work, although most of their work is now done from a mobile van and they go out and about shoeing horses. At one time, with the farms in the area and the importance of the horse in both agriculture and transport, there would have been enough work to keep them in the village permanently, but today, following the advent of the tractor, they have to travel further afield to find work.

Opposite the forge, on my first visit, I met the Collier brothers, Stuart and Gerald, whose family had been running the bakery and supplying Branscombe with bread for the last 125 years. Another thatched building, it was surrounded by piles of wood and faggots – bundles of thinnings from the hedgerows – used to fire the ovens. The bakery itself was pungent with the smell of freshly baked bread.

Not only was the atmosphere heavy with the smell of baking, it was also thick with unseen dust from the flour and the wood ash – what today's Health and Safety Officers would have made of it I dread to think – but it certainly caused Gerald Collier to gasp and constantly try to catch his breath. I remember the terrible problems that he posed the then Production Assistant at the station, Sally Twiss nee Rugg, who is now working alongside the Regional Information Officer for the National Trust in Devon, as she helped the inexperienced author edit the Branscombe programme and cut out all the rasping breaths between Gerald's sentences to produce a version of my recording that was listenable to.

Not for the Colliers the mass produced loaves, neatly packaged and presented in supermarket plastic packaging. Here was the 'real' thing-fresh, crusty and mouth watering – temptingly reminding me of those far off London days when my mother would send me out, as a child to meet another Mr Collier (I wonder if it was any relation?) who delivered bread by horse and cart, and I would return with half the crust picked off hoping that she wouldn't notice!

The Colliers at work in Branscombe Bakery.

The wood fired ovens baked the bread in the traditional way and the resultant taste was unbeatable. Up every day of the year, like the farmers, come rain or shine, long before the sparrows had even thought about farting – a phrase culled from my father-in-law – Stuart and Gerald would clean out, then light up the ovens, make up the dough and happily tend to Branscombe's baking needs. Later in the morning Stuart would go off on the delivery round. Outside the smell of woodsmoke hung heavy in the air and you knew that Branscombe's bakers were in business.

The Colliers continued baking until fairly recently and they managed for years by hand, until they 'went mechanised'. They had 'the electric put in', which meant that the dough could be mixed by machine and they could see better what they were doing, but the wood fired ovens remained and things continued virtually unchanged.

However, at the time I visited – I was lucky to obtain an interview with the Colliers as they had only a few days previously sent away a television film crew from Birmingham because as Gerald explained 'They didn't have an appointment' – I knew that the days of the bakery must be numbered. Both of the brothers were in their seventies and when I asked about the future, Gerald prophetically told me "I'm very vexed because when we go Branscombe will be without a baker and it's very difficult to rely on outside people to keep the village supplied."

Not only that, but I knew that it was very unlikely that anyone today would want to take on the Colliers' calling of bakers whose methods had changed little in generations. Sadly Gerald died and the bakery is now closed but when I went to Branscombe I was lucky enough to meet them both and see the bakery working before it became another piece of Devon's rich history.

Further up the main street, reputed to be the longest village street in Devon, in a house set back above the road, I met another living piece of Branscombe history in the big framed shape of Percy Perryman who told me of the days gone by, snug in his warm sitting room whilst outside one of the bitterest nights of the winter turned my car windscreen to an icy glaze. In the corner of the room the television news was showing horrific pictures of the Space Shuttle Challenger disaster in America. Percy seemed to ignore that momentous event – perhaps he couldn't see too well and the sound was turned down – as he told me that he had left school at the age of 12 and had joined his father in growing potatoes on the cliff tops above the village. "We picked seaweed from the rocks on the beach for manure and then took it on panniers on donkeys' backs up to the plots on the middle cliff. Branscombe became noted for its potatoes because of their flavour. That came from the seaweed in the soil. People came from miles around to buy the potatoes and the rest we used to take into Exeter on the donkeys. "What a trip that must have been I thought and what a hard way to earn a living." After we had lifted the potatoes, we planted mangles (swedes and turnips) to feed the donkeys in the winter". Along with the Colliers' bread, Perryman potatoes are no longer, but another man I met had also chosen an equally hard way to make his living in the village.

Over a pint in the Masons' Arms, John Hughes told me about his work as a local fisherman working for eight months of the year off Branscombe's shelving pebble beach. Spider crab and lobster were his stock in trade and a large part of his catch goes via a wholesaler to Spain – John was already in the European market long before it became fashionable to think in EEC terms. He had been working as a fisherman for eighteen years and I quickly learned that it was not the easiest of ways in which to earn your keep. "In the winter months you've only got to have a bit of wind and you can't get off the beach. You've got to winch the boat up and down across the pebbles and in winter it's very tough. In the summer it's better, I take tourists out tripping and mackrel fishing, but in the winter well..." Rather John Hughes than me I thought.

Refreshed by my pint with John Hughes I next called on someone who was one of the most memorable characters that I met in the series, the Bakers' sister, Ivy Collier at her shop and stores. I remember her producing dog eared receipts for goods delivered to the shop years ago and telling me that one of the chief changes she had seen in her long years in charge of the Branscombe village stores was the rise in prices. Wagging a long bony finger at me, rather like some Victorian school mistress, she lectured me on the rise in cost of a gallon of paraffin and how today's prices simply "didn't compare". What Ivy would have made of the 'new fangled' litres I dread to think. The shop bell tingled in the background as we spoke – on the recording – and a customer entered the shop, but Ivy was in full flow. Whether she realised who I was, she was then in her eighties, and that she was going to be on the 'wireless' I'm not sure, although I did my best to explain, but she told me rather wistfully that "There's very few people in the village now that's real Branscombe people" – many of the properties are owned by absentee landlords or what locals call people from 'up country' and used as weekend homes or holiday lets. She went on to say that in the summer months you would be hard put to find a "real Branscombe person" in either of the pubs or on the village streets. She was of course course right and now, several years on from my visit, that must be even more true today.

I met some truly memorable 'real Branscombe people' on my visit and I mourn their passing.

Braunton

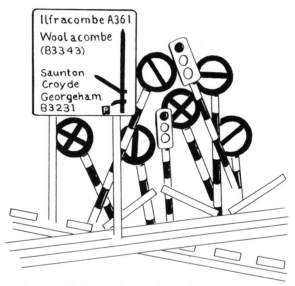

Braunton is one of those places that I knew of, by reputation, long before I visited the village in North Devon. It was perhaps not the sort of reputation of which many would have been proud because I had heard of horrendous traffic jams that choked the main streets during the summer holiday period, as thousands headed to the long sandy beaches that dominate the coastline in this part of Devon.

I decided not to put the stories of the traffic problems in Braunton to the acid test and avoided visiting during the summer and headed there in the middle of February instead. On arriving I recorded what is a familiar radio device – a vox pop or collection of voices to reflect and represent a cross section of local views and opinions. The question that I asked those I stopped on the main through route from Barnstaple to Ilfracombe was 'Is the traffic here a problem?'

"It's really busy in the summer, little kids can't cross the road after school ... it's pretty bad, particularly in the summer ... it's quite busy and trying to get across the road is quite bad ... there's always traffic jams ..."

Just some of the views endorsing what I had heard, which I then put to Derek Holland. At the time he was Chairman of Braunton's Parish Council who are elected to represent Braunton's population of over 8,000. This leads to another claim to fame of which Braunton is more proud than its traffic, that of being the undisputed largest village, not only in Devon but, in the country.

Derek told me – "There's a lot of hold ups in the village, because all the heavy traffic from the industrial estate has to go through the village and all the through traffic coming from Barnstaple or going to the large housing estate at Saunton all travels across that central cross roads. There has been a plan for a by pass since the 1940's which would divert the traffic and this is now being looked at in more detail but it has caused a great deal of controversy in the village."

Local controversy is food and drink to a radio reporter and I asked him to tell me more.

"There is a faction against the original idea of a by pass because this skirted the edge of The Great Field, which is a fairly well known place" (The Great Field is one of the last surviving examples of ancient 'strip farming' left in the country and measures some 365 acres) "and there is concern about what damage, if any, would be caused to The Great Field. Recently the strips have become amalgamated and are now farmed by modern methods and the proposed by-pass would only skirt this field. But I think that some people are of the opinion that the by-pass would actually go through the middle of the Field and destroy something historic and this is where the confusion has come in."

What has happened to Braunton's traffic problems and The Great Field since my visit I don't know but it was clear from talking to Derek Holland that no solution was going to please everybody.

Even with its claim to be the largest village in the country the sheer range of facilities – the village boasts three schools, whereas many villages don't even have one – and shops is overwhelming and it seemed as if whatever you wanted could be had within the village without the need to travel elsewhere. The other thing that struck me very forcibly, which made Braunton different from so many other places that I visited, was the number of young people about. In spite of the traffic Braunton was obviously very much alive and well.

The Braunton Great Field.

Climatically Braunton is also favoured as Jane Hartnoll, a local farmer's wife told me in their sheep barn as she was helping out with the lambing. "It's sheltered and we get warmer winters than a lot of places in Devon, although we have more than our fair share of rain", which is true of many areas in the county, one of the reasons that Devon is such a rich dairy area where the grass grows lush and rich. "In fact," Jane continued, "we are going to have to replant much of our winter corn which has got ruined by the wind and the rain, but we don't get much snow and frost here."

My visit to Jane's farm was memorable not only because of meeting a jolly woman whom one couldn't imagine the weather getting down, but because of her providing me with slabs of delicious home made cake and cups of steaming sweet tea in the farmhouse kitchen, some of the generous Devon hospitality that I encountered nearly everywhere.

Farming is an important industry around the village although at one time the sea was very important too. Today it brings the holiday maker but at one time Braunton had been important as a sea going port as Len Baglole, who runs the cycle shop in the centre of the village, told me.

"Back in the days before the war you had a lot of cargoes brought in here and also loaded away. Before my time iron ore was the thing and Braunton owned a lot of vessels. In fact you know there was more ships owned here than at Appledore and they traded all over from the South Coast to the Continent. When I left school, here in Braunton, I went to sea on a ketch that used to travel up and down the Bristol Channel. She traded in grain and flour but we used to load gravel up for Bristol because all the gravel for the docks at Bristol and Cardiff came from here and then we'd load cargoes like flour and grain back. It was the war that killed off that trade and road transport getting better. In 1935, when I went to sea, I should think that over 100 people then earned their living from going to sea but all that's died out now and Braunton has really changed. In they days you could walk along the main street and know everybody. Today you walk along and you don't know anybody. We were more of a close knit community then, you'd always have a neighbour or someone who would give you a hand if anything happened but that's gone now.."

So too have the ships that Len spoke of. Instead overhead there's the roar of R.A.F. jet planes from nearby Chivenor and in the village itself, even in the middle of winter when I visited, the constant hum of traffic. There's not a lot of point sometimes in looking back at days gone by because often it can be through rose coloured spectacles and you imagine without much difficulty that things were somehow better. In Braunton's case I think they must have been and I would happily swop the traffic and the jets for Len's ships and would loved to have seen Braunton's Great Field being farmed in the strip farming way. There are compensations of course but life in Braunton today is certainly very different from when Len Baglole was a boy.

Broadhembury

Much like a visit to Clovelly, arrival in the East Devon Village of Broadhembury is like stepping back in time. The white cob and thatched cottages flank the main street which runs away from the church at its head with the village pub, the Drewe Arms, sitting back tucked away almost out of sight, although not out of the mind of this book's illustrator who swears that it serves one of the best pints of beer for miles around. Broadhembury is often featured on calendars or the top of chocolate box collections and rightly so because visually it is stunning in its simple beauty – another Devon village that time forgot and taking a moment to pause by the ford at the opposite end of the village to the church the running water can be the only apparent sign of life here for it has a curious, sleepy almost deserted feel to it by day and one wonders if people actually live in these perfect picture post card houses.

They do of course, and most of them share the same landlord who owns most of the property in Broadhembury, Walter Drewe. I met him in the elegant drawing room of his imposing house which is set back from the road in the centre of the village. He explained the history of family ownership.

"The Grange estate owned the whole valley and the village was sold up in 1903. It was my grandfather who bought up a large part of Broadhembury and some of the land. Subsequently my father bought several more houses in the village and now with one or two exceptions the main part of the village is owned by the family. It was my father whose policy it was to preserve the character of the village during his lifetime and to keep the thatch, whilst at the same time modernising the insides of the cottages and houses and I tried to keep that policy going." A visit to Broadhembury will confirm Walter Drewe's success.

The Drewe policy has meant that Broadhembury and its beautiful tranquility has been preserved for both modern day residents and visitors alike to enjoy and it is not uncommon to find, as I did on my visit, a painter hard at work over his or her easel trying to capture some of Broadhembury on canvas or artist's sketch pad.

Walter Drewe told me that a large part of the village's population is retired – perhaps this accounts for the general feel of the place – so what would happen if I wanted to move to the village? I asked. "Was there a waiting list?"

"It varies, most of the property here is let to tenants. There are very few private houses left. They change hands from time to time but not very often." Something told me that even when they did I wouldn't be able to afford the asking price!

Leaving Walter Drewe's house I made my way to the Church. Although he had told me that the village attracts a large number of visitors, here there are no signs of the usual West Country tourist trappings – ice cream vans, cream tea parlours or souvenir shops. I have no doubt that Mr Drewe is responsible for making sure that these don't rear their ugly heads and had they been present they would I'm sure have drawn a very different reaction from the artist I found at work under the trees near the pub. "I used to think of Devon from a coastal point of view, but then I found out that if you drove inland you discovered all these remote little places that really are delightful." I smiled inwardly to myself – they could have been my words.

A Broadhembury street scene from days gone by.

The day I visited Broadhembury to record the programme was one of those glorious spring days, after a particularly harsh winter, when the sun beat down and felt hot enough to burn. In spite of a winter cold or flu which still hung on persistantly, it was something of a relief to slip into the cool of the church where Basil de-Rusett, the organist was practising a hymn, The Rock of Ages, coincidentally composed by a former rector of Broadhembury parish.

This was too good an opportunity to miss and I asked him to repeat the hymn having taken a sound meter reading and this subsequently featured in the programme (a little difficult to re-produce here!). As I admired the church, Basil told me how the roof timbers had been plastered in until the thirteenth century and then in the process of restoration work, in a bid to try and stop the advance of the dreaded death watch beetle, the timbers had been exposed and a painted vine design discovered which Basil belives to be quite unique. With the false ceiling long having gone, Broadhembury Church has a feeling of great space with an unusually lofty roof.

At the time of my visit, Gordon Persey was Chairman of the Parish Council and I drove to his farm just outside the village to meet him. Often during the series of programmes these Parish worthies or elders were a fount of great wisdom and knowledge having lived in the particular village most of their lives. Gordon was no exception.

"The days when the cottages in the village were occupied by farm labourers are long past. Socially it's quite a different place today compared with what it used to be. There used to be a thriving football and cricket team here, but they've faded away. Youth clubs have been tried in recent years, but the young population is just not available now. Younger people don't live in the village because of the difficulty in getting employment and the cost of travelling to where employment is available. Even the family farms are slowly dying out. The school, along with the church, are the focal points of the village. The school though draws its numbers from neighbouring parishes, only half the children come from the village, which means that it's difficult to interest the few young people here in activities after school."

It's hard to see how this situation might change and for me there was a certain sadness in what Gordon had to tell me and explained why although Broadhembury is certainly one of the prettiest Devon villages that I profiled, it does seem to lack some of the life that I have found elsewhere in the county.

Broadwoodwidger

The idea of the radio series was to 'cover' the county and bring a little of the flavour of life in North Devon to the East and the South to the West. It meant many hundreds, if not thousands of miles driving and one of the farthest-'flung' villages I went to was Broadwoodwidger, a place that took some care in pronunciation.

It is about ten miles from Launceston, on the county border with Cornwall and has a population of just over 500 within its parish boundary. At the time I went there, which was early on in the series, the main pre-occupation was water, not that the annual rainfall figure was higher in Broadwoodwidger than in other parts of Devon, but that the South West Water Authority had plans, already well advanced by then, to construct a new reservoir in the area.

It has become something of a standing joke that in spite of heavy rainfall, it appears to take only a very short time without rain for the Water Authority to threaten customers with a cut in supply and worse, the prospect of standpipes in the streets. I first moved to Devon to live in 1976, just after one of the hottest and driest summers in living memory. I can well remember on one occasion as we drove down to the West Country from the more affluent, in terms of water, South East, that the lush green rolling fields that I had come to know and love, had given way to scorched, parched brown fields more reminiscent of the plains of Ethiopia than some of the best dairy farming country in the United Kingdom.

There were those who thought that the fields would never recover, that many trees would be lost forever and farmers literally had a daily battle to get water to stock so that they could survive the incessant heat. The problem of supply, particularly during the summer months is perhaps a direct result of Devon's beauty. Every year the county's population swells as holiday makers flood in (no pun intended) and demand begins to outstrip supply. The root cause of the problem we are told by South West Water is insufficient storage capacity, although there are those who wonder if the solution doesn't lay in the outdated system of distribution and getting the water to where it is needed most.

However, South West Water had determined that it was a question of supply and demand, and that the supply problems would be solved by the construction of new reservoir. In an area of outstanding natural beauty, wherever they chose to site the new facility, they would have run into opposition, even given that this was all taking place long before environmental and green issues became of such great concern. I can't comment on the choice of Broadwoodwidger as the proposed site as I don't know what the alternatives might have been but residents felt that the parish, whose history can be traced back to the eighth century, was under threat.

By 1100, the village had become known as Broadwood its name perhaps reflecting the type and area covered by trees in those times. With the arrival of the Widger family, one of whom, Henry was a great benefactor to the village and parish, the name evolved to what it is today, Broadwoodwidger.

When I was there the village, which has a lovely Norman church, three chapels, a school and a post office, was perhaps unique in having no pub or village hall. Don Porter and Wendy Proutt felt strongly that without either of these, or a village shop, it was difficult to get to know people and although there had been an attempt around the time of the last war to raise funds to build a hall, the interest had dwindled and now people travelled out of the parish to shop and for their 'social life'.

Perhaps part of the problem is the diverse and scattered nature of the population but certainly one thing that did bring them together and everybody shared concern over was the Water Authority's reservoir plans. Although the start of construction was some years off, there were already some nine or ten houses which stood empty and were almost derelict. They had been bought by South West Water in preparation for the start of building and the impending impact had already been felt on village life.

Robert Stratton told me that opposition to the scheme, which will flood some 800 acres within the parish, had been really fierce. "It dropped on this parish, out of the blue, some ten years ago. We were stunned and shocked. It hit everybody like a bombshell but after ten years of debate and discussion and two public enquiries, the minister has given his permission for the reservoir to be built. Much as we might not want it, it's coming to Broadwoodwidger."

After years of opposition, archaeological and photographic surveys on what would be submerged by the new reservoir and a mixture of bitterness on the one hand and resignation on the other by local people, work at last started on the construction and some eighteen years after the plans for 'Roadford' were unveiled to Broadwood-widger, just before Christmas in 1989, the then Minister of State for the Environment came to Devon to 'turn on the taps' to start the process of filling up the new reservoir. When it's full it will supply Plymouth and North Devon and will I'm sure alleviate many, if not all, of Devon's water supply problems, but at what cost to Broadwoodwidger? In human and physical terms it will perhaps never be possible to evaluate what has happened in this scattered rural community and life here will never be the same again. Progress? I'm not sure. What I do know is that I was there BEFORE it happened and I can never again go to turn on the tap without thinking of the sadness of those that I met in the small village of Broadwoodwidger.

Roadford Reservoir under construction.

In the long term, besides the benefits it should bring to the rest of the county, the Roadford Reservoir might bring advantages to Broadwoodwidger. People visiting to see the construction, fishing, walking or spending time here but I wonder if they will pause, like me, and realise that perhaps the local people didn't want it there in the first place? Since the profile of Broadwoodwidger was first broadcast life has changed completely, dramatically and like a tap which has a faulty washer the drip, drip, drip of water is incessant. The local people can't simply take out a spanner to fix it, the drip is there forever and the big bucket to collect the drips, Roadford is a permanent fixture on the landscape. Broadwoodwidger has changed, forever.

Chagford

This chapter is not so much a profile of Chagford as it is today but rather a look back through childhood eyes at how the village was when I was a small boy, although on several return visits, at least one with my portable tape recorder, little seems to have changed from how I remember it.

In the late fifties/early sixties, when the Smiths used to live in London, every year for about four or five years we used to climb into my parents' grey Morris Oxford saloon, a great tank of a car, and head to the West Country to spend a week in Devon and follow this by a week in Cornwall. In those far off days, Devon might as well have been the other side of the world and indeed it seemed to take many hours to arrive at the small Dartmoor village of Chagford and the family run guest house where we stayed. We must have driven my mother and father mad because having barely pulled out of our driveway the squabbling between us children – there were four – would have started and the repeated whining question every few minutes would have been asked – "How long until we get there?" a question I and many others are only too familiar with today. I'm sure that my two young children as we have driven across France for our holidays believe, as we did then, that their father is involved in some sort of conspiracy to drive as slowly as possible, take the longest available route and spend as long as can be engineered to arrive at our destination!

However, after about ten hours – probably with several enforced 'loo breaks' – we would make it to the Beverley Hotel, run by Major Hughes and his wife. I am still to this day deeply impressed by staying somewhere run by a major, it all seemed terribly grand and very grown up despite the fact that I was probably only about six or seven when we first visited Chagford.

I can actually remember little of the major and would be hard put to describe what he looked like. This is probably because what I do recall is that he seldom seemed to be there always claiming to be away fishing for trout at a nearby reservoir although we boys had our suspicions that he was really engaged on some secret army mission, working undercover somewhere in the middle of Dartmoor – quite what we thought he was doing I don't know but it all greatly added to the romance of our holidays.

I can remember vividly two occupants of the Hotel both of whom were called Miss Marshall. They were two elderly spinster type ladies who seemed distant, very old, in fact verging on the ancient, but interested in us children and how we spent our days. They also seemed deeply impressed by the common sense I displayed in walking around, even into the dining room, with a hank of washing line attached to my belt – "In case of having to rescue people off the moors or from down mine shafts" I explained, which they seemed to accept as a most sensible and wise precaution.

Chagford in those days was a quiet sleepy little backwater – try parking on the town or village square in the summer today – and obviously very different from life as we knew it in London. Although I saw horses, the local baker had one and my mother seemed regularly to take us to see the Horseguards in Whitehall on a number 3 bus – it wasn't until I went to Chagford that I actually got very close to one let alone learned to ride.

Mr French who ran the riding stables where we were deposited to take off with him on treks across the moors in the Fernworthy direction was a great character. In the height of summer he dressed in gaiters, big brown shiny boots, fawn coloured flannel trousers, a yellow checked waistcoat with a trilby hat perched permanently on his head. When the weather turned to rain he donned an enormous well worn faded cream coloured trench coat which enveloped both him, his saddle and the horse's withers. Looking back had he appeared on the radio, I would probaly have had to severely edit some of his verbal instructions to us as he taught us the basics of riding – his language could be be somewhat direct! However he taught us well how to sit on a horse without falling off at a canter and even how to leave go of the saddle as his ponies took off, almost on auto pilot, across the moorland.I recall that his way of encouraging me to leave go was to ride alongside me hitting my hands with his riding crop until I released the pommel and gripped the reins until my fingers turned white, but once learned never forgotten.

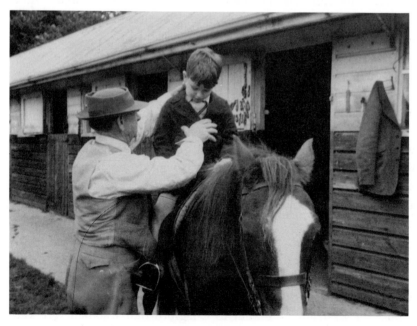

The author, as a boy, being taught to ride by Mr French.

One memory of Mr French, which deeply impressed my father, was the day that we had offered to take him to the Princetown horse sales. (Little did I realise in those days the ultimate fate of those delightful Dartmoor ponies knocked down at auction to a crowd of Mr French 'look alikes'.) On meeting Mr French outside the Three Crowns or where ever the 'pick up point' was the sun shone from a cloudless blue sky. Mr French however had his trusty trench coat draped over his arm. "It'll be rain by dinner time" he said as he climbed in, smelling strongly of horse and sure enough he was right. By the time we left the horse sale the mists had come down and that thin persistent Dartmoor drizzle had arrived. Ah the wisdom of Devon folk, as we shivered in our artex short sleeved shirts. We 'townies' knew nothing of life in the country.

If Mr French was a character, then Webbers, the shop on the town square was the eighth wonder of the world. The place was an Aladdin's cave, the Harrods of Chagford. It seemed to stock everything from newspapers to roof racks, from paint and tools to clothing – a paradise for small boys whose prime interests in life were sheath knives and fishing hooks. Returning there today it is still the same and I'm sure that like Harrods if they haven't got it – which is most unlikely – then they can get it for you.

The holidays in Chagford came to an end for which, looking back, I blame Rolf Harris, although to be fair it wasn't entirely his fault that those lazy summer days spent riding, fishing at Fingle Bridge where my sister spent all her time disentangling snagged line from rocks for us and my father tried to change the subject when I told a water bailiff that I had just caught a trout – we didn't have a permit at the time – and walking the moors with Eric Hemery, an expert and renowned guide, drew to a natural close. We grew up and ventured abroad for our holidays, me little dreaming that one day I would return to live and work in the county of my youth.

Rolf Harris was a larger than life character that we all recognised from being on our newly acquired television set back in London. In those days he appeared on children's programmes with a character called Olly the Octopus painted on his hand, his first finger and thumb forming Olly's mouth telling you what programme followed.

Rolf Harris was there, in person at the Guest House and not only that he was camping on the lawn. We all thought this terribly brave and I can remember evenings spent in awe of this man who genuinely seemed pleased by the attention we gave him, although I'm sure in reality he found it all a bit trying, and Rolf Harris became a big part of the magic of those holidays of long ago in Chagford.

He was there 'stepping out' with Major and Mrs Hughes daughter, Alwen, whom he subsequently married. The Beverley closed down, although I'm not sure that the two events were related, and we never returned there as a family favouring such exotic locations as Austria instead. Today the Beverley Hotel is no longer a guest house, but on return visits to Chagford I have been known to sneak in, up their drive – it's now some sort of retirement home – and look with misty eyes on the lawn where we met Rolf Harris, across to the majestic sweep of the foothills of Dartmoor where, as we learned with Mr French, the weather can change in a moment, dream of the trout that got away, marvel that Webbers is still bursting at the seams with stock of all descriptions and that as a young boy I was a small part of all this and as an adult I am lucky enough to have come back to Devon and can make irregular visits back in time to the Chagford of all those years ago.

Clovelly

Sheila Ellis, who has lived in this North Devon coastal village all her life, told me that for her "There's no-where else quite like Clovelly," and if you have never been there it's difficult to appreciate exactly what she means. Charles Kingsley best summed the place up when he wrote in 1849 on returning there – "I cannot believe my eyes; the same place, the pavement... it is as if I was a little boy again, or the place had stood still while all the world had been rushing and rumbling past it..."

Clovelly, where time has stood still, is about ten miles along the spectacular and often wild coastline from Bideford. Here you won't find yourself in danger of being knocked down by the all invading motor car, for cars are banned from the village's streets and to explore the delights that Clovelly has to offer you have to leave your car in the car park at the top and take to Shank's pony. The houses cluster tightly together either side of the main cobbled street called Up-Along or Down-Along, depending on which way you are walking. When I was last there it was the middle of winter, a crisp clear blue sky with the smell of woodsmoke in the air and closing your eyes, it was easy to imagine yourself caught in a time warp with the modern trappings and pace of life left far behind. Perhaps in summer it's a different tale when Clovelly bustles with the thousands of visitors who descend on the village from all over the world to experience its charm.

Entering the village from the car park, despite the magnificent view of the bay below, you have little idea of what delights await you. With the New Inn on your right you begin the descent to Clovelly's small harbour and one of the first things that I noticed was the sledges laying outside, or leaning up against, the houses. Practical devices these for transporting the necessities of life from top to bottom of the village. There's no sign of telephone or electricity cables overhead, all the mains services are taken underground and the village is immaculately clean and tidy.

Sheila Ellis told me – "The oldest part of the village is in Higher Clovelly where the farms date back to 1200, but the village of Clovelly as we know it today is about 400 years old. George Carey was the owner then and he had the stream which ran down the hill diverted, cobbles brought up from the pier and laid on the river bed which accounts for why our main street is so winding from top to bottom."

In the middle of the village there's a Post Office and shop and they too, like the villagers, have to bring down their supplies on sledges. The only exception to the no traffic rule is the ambulance, should it be needed, which has to reverse down the steep High Street, and drive back up over the cobbles – not a journey that I'd be keen to undertake. Donkeys were used at one time for transport with panniers of herring caught by Clovelly's fishermen strapped across their backs, but now they only work for six months of the year to carry luggage and laundry for the New Inn and of course pose for the holidaymakers' photographs with children.

Perched on the hillside the sound and smell of the sea is never far away as Trevor Davey explained – "The sea is Clovelly, Clovelly is the sea really. In the past it was a very busy fishing village and our herrings were famous throughout the county. It was essentially small boat fishing, but it bred very good seamen known throughout the West Country and the World."

Clovelly Harbour at the turn of the century.

The herring has all but disappeared from off this rugged coast where the groundswell from the Atlantic can lash and batter the harbour walls and the wind tear in from the sea, both frightening in their ferocity. Given the nature of the sea and there being no land, save Lundy Island between Clovelly and America, it's more than a little perplexing that the village's lifeboat house now stands empty having fallen victim to re-organisation. Percy Shackson, an eldery man when I met him, had been involved with the lifeboat, when the village had one, since the age of 17. Percy 'sneaked' onto the 12 handed rowing boat before he should have been allowed to, eighteen was the age for joining the crew.

Although they had a sail and often relied on wind power, the wind could be in the wrong direction and many times they returned with sore hands from a rescue mission, and on one occasion came back with a hole three feet by two feet ripped in the bottom of the boat where it had been thrown back onto the beach twice before they could launch it. Percy was involved in saving over 100 people from the cruel clutches of the sea and was awarded the Royal Lifeboat Institution's Life Saving medal which he proudly sported in his lapel.

Percy's son, Graham, left Clovelly having spent 26 years living in the village but he reckons that "When you've lived in Clovelly you can go away and perhaps forget about the place. Then, all of a sudden, it comes back to you, what a wonderful place it is. It's all about families and companionship, for me that sums Clovelly up." Perhaps that's the reason that he's back living there now.

Harry Clement wasn't really a newcomer, as he'd been evacuated to Clovelly in the last war. "I'd seen nothing like it before coming from London as I did." He remembers the warmth of the welcome that he and others like him got in those days and after a career with the Metropolitan Police he returned to live in the village again." Clovelly was always my home. I'd been accepted as one of their sons. I've seen some marvellous places as my professional life took me throughout the world but none of them come within an inch of Clovelly."

It's this feeling of a place whose reputation has gone before it that strikes me too about the place. Clovelly is like Venice, a place that I had longed to visit and on going there more than lived up to expectation. Your mind's eye conjurers up a picture perhaps dimly remembered from photographs and on arrival it's all there, just as you had expected.

Over the years the village has changed very little physically, although there are few of the orginal families that still survive today. It's a very special place, as Sheila Ellis said "There's no-where in the world like it", a sentiment echoed by Alan Johns a former chairman of the Parish Council – "I'm a Clovelly man, and always will be. Once you lived in Clovelly, you never forget it". The same is true of a visit here.

Drewsteignton

As you will have read in the section on Chagford, it was to this beautiful area on the edge of Dartmoor that we used to come for part of our summer holidays and Drewsteignton was almost as much a part of those long gone days as was Chagford itself. Below the village lies one of Devon's most famous, and lovely, tourist spots, Fingle Bridge. This granite packhorse crossing over the River Teign has really not changed one scrap since we used to come over 30 years ago to fish, paddle and scramble from rock to rock. Perhaps there are more people today but the bridge itself has changed little if at all and is one of those places that you can conjure up in vivid detail, with absolutely no effort, so clearly is it etched on your sub-conscious. I love the place.

The landlady of the Drewe Arms hasn't changed either. Aunt Mabel Mudge has been there since 1919. In 1988, the most recent occasion I visited her, armed with my tape recorder, it was her ninety-third birthday. She took it all very much in her stride talking to me again, after all she had just been interviewed for a 'real' Down

Your Way programme for Radio 4 and by a television film crew so someone from Radio Devon was chicken feed to an old 'pro' like her.

I had met her several years previously and had been ushered in for an audience with her in her cosy kitchen cum sitting room at one end of the pub. Then, as with the visit on her birthday I was struck by the sight of this frail old lady, propped up on one end of the sofa, who has been landlady at the Drewe Arms for years, long before I first came to Devon. Aunt Mabel's hearing wasn't so good , but her watery eyes had a wicked sparkle and certainly her memory was anything but faded.

I asked her about the changes that she'd seen take place in Drewsteignton – "Some of it's alright, but some I think would be far better off if it was as it was. Times have changed. You can't compare it today with how it was years ago. All the prices, I mean to say today everything is so expensive." There's little concession to some of the modern pub trappings in the Drewe Arms. Mabel wouldn't tolerate a juke box or a fruit machine to boost trade – "Oh no, I'm not going to be worried by none of that. Weekends as a rule we has us a little sing song, all merry and bright, and that'll do me."

Like much else in Devon, I took time to ponder, what will happen to the pub when Mabel goes? There is no possibility that she could ever be replaced and time inevitably will march on and the Drewe Arms will change and it won't be for the better. Reckoned to be the oldest landlady in the country Aunt Mabel is unique. The last time we met was when I was doing a special Christmas programme for the BBC and I was saddened to see how much she had aged since our previous encounter. She did manage to recall how at Christmas the Drewsteignton baker allowed people to carry their roasting tins to the bakery where he'd slide them into his ovens for a few pennies and cook their Christmas meal. Aside from this Mabel seemed more pre-occupied with a fear of being broken into – a phobia shared by many of the elderly – and it was soon clear that she was either unable, or not in the mood, to recall much about Christmas in the village. It can only be a matter of time...

Drewsteignton has another old resident, or rather former resident, whose fame spreads far beyond the village itself. 'Ma' is featured in the Guiness Book of Records, in the Mammals and Birds section! Recorded as the oldest cat in Britain Ma, a tabby, owned by Mrs Alice St. George Moore of Drewsteignton was put to sleep in November 1957 at the age of 34. It would seem that there is another contender for the honour of the oldest 'Puss', a cat named exactly that who was also a tabby and came from Clayhidon in East Devon. It must be something about the quality of mice in the county!

Jack Price's family connection with the village goes back further than Mabel has been in the pub, to before 1897. It was Queen Victoria's Diamond Jubilee Year when Jack's grandmother opened up a tea room at Fingle Bridge to cater for the tourists who came to the village and the area, even in those days. Jack was able to quote the price of a 'real' tea served in his grandmother's time when the menu consisted of ham and tongue, pickle and salad, a home made roll and butter followed by a cream tea of buns and clotted cream, with bread and butter and jam ending up with fruit and cream all washed down with a pot of tea for half a crown! No wonder Mabel had told me that she thought everything so expensive today.

The Anglers' Rest at the turn of the century.

Fingle Bridge Tea Shelter
(CATERERS)
DREWSTEIGNTON - Nr. Exeter

Menu

I
BREAD & BUTTER, CAKE & JAM
1/2 per head

II
As above with CUTROUNDS & CREAM
1/6 per head

III
As No. II. with FRUIT & CREAM
2/- per head

IV
HAM & BEEF
SALAD & SAUCES
BREAD & BUTTER, CAKE & JAM
CUTROUNDS & CREAM
:: 2/6 ::

J. ASHPLANT, Proprietor

Now it's the third generation of Jack's family, his son and daughter running the Angler's Rest at the bridge, but Jack retains his connections with the village. He recalled the story of the Drewsteignton Home Guard during the last war, who used to mount a watch on top of the church tower, no doubt fortified by a tot from the pub which is next door. Jack takes up the tale. "Tom Ashplant, who is a relation of mine, was on duty one night. Well he was the village postmaster and he had to come down early from his watch so as to meet the mail van. Tom was a bit stout, and with his great coat on with a ground sheet on top of that, he had difficulty getting down the narrow spiral staircase of the tower. The trick to overcome this was to take off your coat and sheet, hurl it from off the top of the tower onto the footpath below and collect it when you got to the bottom. On one particular morning it was a bit breezy and Tom's great coat got caught up on the minute hand of the church clock just before six o'clock. It took the minute hand right round to six thirty so advancing the church clock by half an hour. Well Drewsteignton people swear by the church clock and as people were getting ready to go off to work on the farms and in the quarry, the announcer on the wireless was telling them it was seven o'clock they knew he was wrong as the village clock had struke seven half an hour previously. Tom created pandemonium in the village that morning and the rector nearly banned the Home Guard from the tower."

The church tower survived that test of time alongside the pub and Fingle Bridge but it will be interesting to see if nearby Castle Drogo survives a similar test. The Castle is a mock castellated version of what traditionally is described as a castle and now in the hands of the National Trust it enjoys both beautiful grounds and a superb situation off a road above the village itself. Indeed the whole area is rich in natural beauty and abounds in walks justly known far beyond Devon's boundaries.

If things are much the same outwardly in Drewsteignton as they have been for centuries then beyond the doors and windows of the mostly cob and thatched houses things have changed quite a bit according to Henry Scott who has lived there all his life. "The old families have died out considerably and there's been a big take over of people coming in from away and buying up the available cottages. I think that it's one of these things that's taken place throughout Devon – it's general really and I don't know that there's much that be done to alter it."

That may be true and although my eyes and memory tell me that little has changed in Drewsteignton since I first went there as a boy, I'm sure that underneath it's a very different place. Nevertheless it's still picturesque and as I indicated earlier, I love it and I know that it was a great thrill for my parents to retrace their steps with my wife, Lucy, and our young son Ben and make a return visit a few years ago to the village. Drewsteignton is a place that I shall never get tired of.

Gittisham

Gittisham is another village that features large in my own private life, for it was here at Combe House Hotel that I spent the night before my wedding, or some of it anyway. At Combe House, formerly the estate manor house, now a magnificent country hotel, my parents gave both my and my wife to be Lucy's, family an enormous banquet on the evening before the wedding itself.

Following an outing to various pubs in the vicinity with the best man and a collection of friends who had arrived in Devon for the occasion, along with calling in at nearby Honiton Motel for a disco, Fergus my noble best man escorted me back to the hotel, driving his mother's car, borrowed for the weekend. Unhappily on the way back we were forced to swerve off the hotel driveway to avoid a pig who crossed it seemed quite deliberately in front of the car. In spite of showing excellent car control and driving skill, Fergus managed to drive the car over a large tree stump, left thoughtlessly in our path by someone, and the result was a cracked chassis which did little to please Fergus's mother when the car was pronounced a write off by the insurance company. Our difficulties were far from over however because when we got to the hotel itself, we found the building locked and ourselves locked out.

To this day the owners of the hotel do not know how we got in and I am not about to 'spill the beans' here, but suffice it to say that in spite of having had only it seemed about ten minutes sleep, being subjected to a grilling by the family and the hotel staff over breakfast, whilst being urged by my Aunt Ethel to eat a hearty meal, we never cracked under interrogation, although my stomach almost gave way under the onslaught of kippers, toast and marmalade.

Following Aunt Ethel's instructions I ate the breakfast of a condemned man before sliding off to nurse my hangover. So the village of Gittisham and Combe House with its excellent food passed into the folk lore story of my wedding and although a lot more happened that weekend in Devon some fifteen years ago that, as they say, is another story.

Gittisham has cropped up several times since our marriage. Although I have never had the pleasure of eating there again, Combe House was the base for one of the most remarkable people in Devon that it has ever been my fortune to meet, Clive Essame. Clive is crippled and walks with great difficulty, often with the help of a stick or crutches. I first met him when I was market gardening, something that my wife and I did for some six years, and Clive came to look at the polythene tunnels in which we were growing vegetables. Clive had negotiated with the Boswells, who ran Combe House, to start a herb garden centre in the hotel's walled garden and wanted advice on what equipment to get.

I was flattered that he should have come to ask my advice, being a mere novice in the field as it were, but I can remember I was also greatly impressed that he was even considering, given his physical handicap, taking on such a project. But, take it on he did and over the period that he was running it we took friends there to buy herbs from him and we used to see him on his stall in the nearby market. Clive and his herb enterpise, along with his wife who worked just as hard as he did, were even featured in one of the 'quality' Sunday Magazine supplements. But in spite of my very occasional patronage, there is after all a limit to how many herbs can be grown in one garden, and the attention of the national media Clive couldn't make the herb garden pay and it folded.

The next time I saw him was at an exhibition in a local library where he was manning a stall offering advice and training to handicapped and disadvantaged people and he didn't seem to have changed a bit. Perhaps he was a little more crippled and less mobile than before but in spite of all that was his normal cheerful self whom I had come to know slightly when he ran the herb garden. I haven't seen him for some time now but was reminded of him again just before last Christmas. I was in his brother's 'Farm Shop' – an enterprising lot these Essames – when I saw a delightful colour photograph on a greeting card. On picking it up I realised that it was

Gittisham today.

a picture of Gittisham and on turning it over saw that it has been taken by none other than, yes you've guessed it, Clive Essame. If only at times when I feel low, tired or exhausted I could recall Clive's example I would stop feeling sorry for myself. His spirit, guts and sheer determination, not to mention his constant good humour, should be an example to us all and most of all to me. I hope that if he reads this he won't feel too embarrased, but he really is a remarkable man.

No less remarkable really is the story of another young man who lives in Gittisham, Richard Marker. In the Profile of this tiny, thatched East Devon village he told me his story. The village is largely owned by the Marker family and Rosemary Marker first sketched in the family background for me. "The Markers inherited the estate from the Rector of nearby Aylesbeare. At that time it was very large and included land not only in Devon, but also in Dorset and Somerset, all in all about thirteen thousand acres. Today owing to death duties etc it's down to about four thousand acres." Well I thought, that's no mean area of land, just imagine being owner and 'squire' of that lot. Well that's what Richard Marker now is. He takes up the story...

"Rosemary Marker's husband is my mother's first cousin and the estate has come down to me through my mother's side of the family. When I was thirteen years old, living in Canada, I was told about the estate and that was the first I had heard of Gittisham, but it didn't really mean very much to me. But when I was eighteen, I came over for a visit and stayed with Rosemary for about two weeks but it didn't really sink in that one day this would be mine. When I turned twenty one, it sank in though, because I actually inherited the estate then and had to change my name from Richard Trewlany which was my real name. I thought it was very nice, but I was living my life in Canada had my job and was quite happy there. It was extremely difficult when we arived. Our first year here we didn't really enjoy that much, although Rosemary tried to make things easier for us by trying to introduce us to people we didn't really start to enjoy living here until we got out and made our own friends and I started working on the estate."

Richard today is not so much the local squire but describes himself as 'caretaker' of the estate, looking after it for his children and his children's children, and in spite of his still very pronounced accent, which is definitely anything but Devonian, he and his wife, Nelly, have settled happily into Gittisham and its way of life. For many Richard's story would be a dream come true, like a win on the pools. For many it would change their attitude towards others, but in a lot of ways Richard seems strangely unaffected by such a complete change in his life and obviously takes his responsibilities in preserving the character of Gittisham and the estate in the way that the Markers have for years seriously. I think the village is in safe hands.

Hatherleigh

Hatherleigh was a place that somehow I didn't seem able to get away from in one way or another for several years,although I didn't actually go there until quite late on in the series. One of the reasons was that as well as presenting the Village Profile series for BBC Radio Devon, I also presented their weekly farming programme which meant that often I would be speaking to the current Chairman of Devon's National Farmers' Union. One year this was a man called Geoffrey Cleverdon who farmed just outside the town. Although we spoke quite often, it would be in Exeter at the Headquarters of the Devon NFU or at the Radio Devon studios, so when I went to Hatherleigh he was naturally one of the people that I interviewed.

I was also sent to the town by a Producer for the 'You and Yours' programme on Radio Four to do an item on the 'Squire' of Hatherleigh looking to fill the ancient office of town aletaster. This was a job, rather like a current day Trading Standards Officer, where the Squire's Officer or Aletaster would make a tour of inspection of the local public houses sampling their beer and making sure that it was up to required standard – a job which, although I didn't get, was, I felt, right up my street.

Another reason for there being a firm link with Hatherleigh, even prior to my visit was that a man called Dennis Bater was in almost constant touch with Radio Devon on the 'phone in programmes and competitions, almost daily at one time. He also wanted to join the station's Advisory Council and on my Village Profile meeting him was almost like meeting up with an old friend.

Hatherleigh set deep in the heart of North Devon is not so much a village as a town, declared as such by a Royal Charter in 1693. Its history can be traced back for over a thousand years and there are those who will tell you that it is probably the smallest town in the country. There's certainly a farming or agricultural flavour to the place with a busy bustling weekly market held there where auctioneers sell cattle and sheep, talking at high speed in what sounds to me almost like a foreign language but is obviously understood by the shrewd North Devon farmers looking on as stock is bought and sold. Dennis Bater, whom I mentioned earlier, works at the cattle market as a steward or porter.

As well as working at the market, Dennis runs the town's Fish and Chip Shop in the High Street, one of many flourishing town businesses, for here you will find almost any type of shop that you could think of, the town even has its own fire and police stations. The town has a connection with the village of Tetcott, which you will find featured elsewhere in this book, because at one time the town was owned by the Arscott family. When they died out, the Molesworths sold the estate to the Oldham family, predecessors to the present day Lord of the Manor Tim Lang, who rides round his 'manor' on an old push bike sporting bicycle clips.

The old 'courts' who acted as the Lord of the Manor's officers have fallen into disuse, but Tim was keen to revive them as much from a sentimental point of view as from a practical one and hence the search for an aletaster.

Outside the town there is an industrial estate, whilst sited behind the cattle market is an abbatoir, the home of Hatherleigh Meat Ltd run by Peter Bowyer, a traditional business using modern methods to kill and process meat for both the home and the export markets. On the other extreme. from a large highly mechanised industry, in

Hatherleigh you can go to the smaller one man operation like Harry James who makes fitted kitchens, bedrooms and furniture just outside the town, although having outgrown his present premises he was hoping to move into the town itself in the near future.

Hatherleigh from the air just before the last war.

The hardware store, above the town square run by Cecil Ellicott, is one of those old fashioned type places where it seems that you can get almost anything, including the tar that Cecil gets to steep the barrels for the annual Hatherleigh Festival of Fire. Brian Doidge, a huge barrel of a man himself, was in charge of the Hatherleigh Tar Barrel ceremony where every year barrels are coated with several layers of tar, then set alight and dragged flaming on a sledge through the town, a throw back to a pagan superstition and festival to ward off evil spirits. It's a truely terrifying but spectacular event which frightened the life out of me, although my young children thought it all great fun when we went to the Hatherleigh Carnival one year. The town band plays, there's a carnival procession by torchlight and the barrels and if ever you are in the area in November it's a spectacle that has to be seen to be believed.

Geoff Cleverdon, whom I mentioned at the begining of this section is not only a farmer, but also something of a local history expert on Hatherleigh. He farms on the edge of Hatherleigh Moor which as he told me "is an area of approximately four hundred and fifty acres of common land. This means that it's common to those who reside within the 'common boundary' of Hatherleigh. They used to be called 'Potboilers'. It is a term meaning people who literally boil their pot in their own house, as opposed to someone who is a ratepayer or landlord of a property in which they don't live. All have got grazing rights, but of course not everybody excercises them so we have to take stock in from others. It's all regulated and it works very well."

Dennis Bater, who as I said runs the local Fish and Chip shop, and works at the town market is also the Chairman of the Carnival Committee and a lot more besides. He does a post round in the morning and is also a member of the town fire brigade and it seemed quite a natural link for Dennis to tell me about Hatherleigh's water supply, the Buddle. The Buddle is sited just above Dennis's chip shop in a side turning off the main street and he directed me to George Horn to explain more about it. "It's a supply of water coming out from the wall which people think has been running for between two hundred and two hundred and fifty years. My father, and my grandfather before him, told me that the source of the water comes from a well that was dug outside what is now the butcher's shop, not very far out into the road and a pipe was taken from the well, run down under the pavement and comes out where the Buddle is running at the present time. It's always been running there and has never dried up. It gets very slow sometimes in dry weather and when we have had the mains cut off, which we have had, people can get their water from the Buddle." The Hatherleigh Buddle is pictured at the start of this chapter.

In other villages that I have been to people have told tales of getting their water in buckets from the village pumps or wells and in Hatherleigh they still can and do you know that water from the town's Buddle tastes delicious. With burning tar barrels, a hardware shop packed from floor to ceiling with anything that you could possibly need, the old 'Potboilers', the town market, a man who is postman, market porter as well as fireman and fish fryer and its own well, the Buddle, Hatherleigh is a quite remarkable place. I wonder if they've appointed their aletaster yet?

As I write this in January of 1990, having just had my electricity power restored after some five days following some of the most severe gales and storms in living memory I have heard that the storms sent the Hatherleigh church steeple crashing through the church roof and I have seen the pictures of the devastation in the local press. It's very sad and I wish them well with the vast restoration work that will now be necessary.

Hemyock

At the foot of the romantically named Blackdown Hills, on the border between Devon and Somerset, lays the village of Hemyock. The village is much larger than many featured in this book with many of the people who live there finding employment at the large milk factory run by St Ivel.

Like the famous Windmill Theatre, the factory never closes except for Christmas, running round the clock, with a labour force of nearly 250 producing a low fat dairy spread, called St Ivel Gold. Although it is sited in the heart of good dairy country, it's surprising to learn that the milk for processing comes from as far away as Cornwall rather than the local farms. But the product is distributed nationally and the factory is certainly very much a part of life in the village and has been in existence here in one form or another for over a hundred years.

Chris Draycott, who is a retired Detective Chief Superintendent from London, now lives in the village and along with Brian Clist, wrote a commemorative village history, sponsored by St Ivel, to celebrate the centenary of the factory and he told me that writing the book was a great adventure for him: having moved to the village just seven years previously it provided him with a great opportunity of meeting people in the village who he hadn't met before. He also discovered much to his delight that there had at one time been three inns in the village, that an early French bi-plane had been sighted over the village in about 1912 which caused great excitement, and he learnt much about the now renovated castle.

The village is very well off in terms of shops and facilities but Chris strongly maintains that despite its growth Hemyock remains very much a village in feel and atmosphere. But there's little doubt that Hemyock has changed a great deal over the years, particularly within living memory of people like Bill Griffiths, who has lived there all his life. He highlighted one of the major changes that he had seen as the arrival of miximatosis which saw off many of the rabbit population. "At one time it was all rabbits and eggs around here, but when the disease came most of the trappers were out of work and that was a really big change. Like the dairy, when I started there in 1916, we used to do everything by hand, but then that all changed too, it became all mechanised. The milk used to be picked up by lorries with churns, nowadays it's all tankers. At one time there used to be over 700 farmers supplying milk to the factory and my job for about 50 years was to smell the milk and I can tell you during that time I smelled some pretty rotten stuff!"

One thing which is certain is that today the quality of the milk is checked by far more scientific means than relying on Bill's sense of smell. Bill has seen a lot of new building go on in the village and the construction of new estates. "They've destroyed what was once a little village and everything now is semi townie, if you know what I mean. It's very different today, but a lot's gone on here you know. The first eggs were dried here, the first dried milk powder and the first ice cream powder was made in Hemyock – I know, 'cos I was there " he chuckled.

Another aspect of village life that spread far beyond Hemyock was the now national Young Farmers' movement. Brian Clist, who comes from a very long established Devon family and who co-wrote the village history with Chris Draycott, is an expert on the topic and over a fabulous high tea laid on a long farmhouse table at the family home, he told me more.

"The actual Young Farmers' movement was originally called the Calf Club and started in 1920. It was sponsored by the milk factory which was started by four local farmers to produce butter. The founders kept going until they were bought out. At the end of the First World War, there was a tremendous amount of malnutrition, even in country districts, but especially in cities, and the milk side of the business at the factory really took off. The dairy wanted to have as much milk as they could get and someone came up with the brilliant idea of forming the Calf Club."

The start of the Young Farmers – Hemyock Calf Club.

"A Canadian had moved into the village with experience of similar clubs in Canada, where they were known as Four H Clubs, and a letter was sent out to farmers with teenage children in the late winter of 1920. A meeting was called and within a month or so of the meeting the Calf Club was under way. About twenty three youngsters joined, and an equal number of calves purchased and allocated by lot to a child."

I asked Brian if the idea of forming the club was to raise the milk yield over the course of time. "Yes I think it was. Yields hadn't really altered very much for a hundred years or more and were running at about 400 gallons per cow per year. The directors of the factory, anxious to get more milk were faced with encouraging farmers to keep more cows or to improve the quality of the cows that were going to run on their farms. It was interesting too that the first distribution of calves were from stock that was producing more than average milk yeild."

"The children bought the calves for about five pounds a head, which was loaned to them by the factory. After a year the calves were then sold and within a couple of years a nucleus of better quality stock was introduced into the dairy herds around Hemyock and the thing went from there. In the third year the calves brought in were Ayreshires from Scotland which must have been the first time that the breed was seen in Devon." Another first for Hemyock.

The idea was copied in Hampshire and then in Leicestershire and the growth of the movement was fairly rapid from then on and even the national press sat up and took notice – the Daily Mail began to sponsor the Calf Club and in Brian's words "it mushroomed" and grew into the Young Farmers' movement of today.

Thus in the not so small village of Hemyock a truely national farming story has its roots and although today not so many of the inhabitants earn their living from the land, the farming tradition continues and a dairy product which is sold the length and breadth of the country originates in the village.

Luppitt

Take any village in the country and I would defy you to find the combination of the unusual, if not the unique, that you find in the tiny East Devon village of Luppitt. There's the farmer whose front room is turned over to house the village pub, although don't all rush at once to buy a drink at the Luppitt Inn as it would be a real squeeze to fit in. Up the road from the pub is a residential farm for mentally handicapped people. In an isolated house above the village you find the base for an order of Buddhist monks. In addition, Luppitt was then home to a young man who worked as Lighting Designer to some of the top names in the Rock music business like Tina Turner, Mick Jagger and Stevie Wonder and you have an idea of why I think that Luppitt is rather different.

Patrick Woodroffe on tour with Mick Jagger and Tina Turner.

Luppitt is about five miles from the busy market town of Honiton and is known to some of the local people as Luppitt harbour. Rumour has it that a local poacher, having set his mole traps, was somewhat perplexed on returning to them to find that someone had put mackerel in the traps instead of the moles that he expected to find! Perhaps this story explains the unusual title of the local parish magazine, The Luppitt Packet.

Archie Wright used to run the Luppitt Inn and he didn't mind that customers invaded the privacy of his home – just as well given that he has only got two rooms in which they can sup their beer! "It's somewhere for people to come" he told me before he died last year. You couldn't get many of the fancy type drinks that you find in most of the pubs today; Archie catered for the basic needs of his clientele and for my money it's one of the best, most welcoming pubs in the county and it's very sad that Archie is no longer with us.

The Devon Vihara, or Buddhist monastery, is at Odle Cottage overlooking the Otter Valley on the edge of Luppitt Common, a wild spot in the midst of some of the best farming land in the area. The monastery is the home of two monks and two novices, with Brother Kitisaru being the Senior monk. He's shaven headed and when I met him I was privileged to be allowed into the monastery during a time of retreat. He was seated cross legged on floor cushions and there was an instant, incredible sense of peace and well being about the man as he explained to me more about his religious beliefs.

"The word Buddha is a quite simple word meaning 'awake'. Buddhism is a teaching that helps all human beings to wake up to what it means to be a living being on this planet. The teaching encourages all beings to live in a sensitive way, a compassionate way and particularly a mindful way."

The monks are not allowed to possess money, so there is daily contact with the outside world, their supporters supplying them with food and sustenance. How I wondered do they lead their lives?

"We get up at four in the morning and at five o'clock we meet for chanting and devotion and sitting in meditation. The chanting is in an ancient Indian language and basically what we are doing is intending our minds to live today in a wise way, to live today in a truthful way, to live today in a virtuous way. It's like looking at a map in the morning before going on a journey and saying 'Ah that's the way I want to go.' The meditation is a period of quiet thought and prayer."

Why the shaven head? "It's a token of leaving behind the worldly life and inclining towards a spiritual life and the robe that I am wearing is ochre or earthen coloured and is also a symbol of simplicity which is the life style of a monk who has to learn how to live simply and try to set an example that as beings we can be happy and joyful without very much. As far as food is concerned we are delighted to receive what ever is offered – in fact we are dependent on our lay community which inspires us to live in a way which is worthy of support."

It certainly seemed from my brief visit to the monastery that Brother Kitisaru was at peace with both himself and the world and that if ever in my life I have had a real religious experience my visit to the Devon Vihara was it.

Brother Kitisaru.

Equally moving is Greenacres Farm which was founded by David Walker and his wife. The main purpose of Greenacres is to give a home to 11 mentally handicapped adults which is as close as possible to the sort of home circumstances that you or I would live in. In these days when the objective seems to move as many mentally ill or handicapped people back into the community to lead as normal a life as possible Greenacres could be seen as a flagship leading the way in how best this might be achieved. The Walkers have a mentally handicapped son themselves which was the spur to found the unit. "We couldn't see any future for him after being at Lingfield Hospital School, or others like him, so we decided to do something about it ourselves. We tried for many many months to find a suitable property in the South of England and then we had a stroke of luck. We came down to Devon to visit some friends and we saw the details of this place in an estate agents and realised it was the place for us, where we could create a meaningful working week."

When the Walkers moved to Luppitt there was some local opposition to the idea of opening a home for the mentally handicapped, perhaps based on the fear of the unknown – the Does He Take Sugar syndrome. "I think most people here now support us and we have a very strong friends organisation made up entirely of people from the village." The proof of Greenacres is really in visiting the place and seeing David Walker's ideals realised. Admittedly there was an extra air of excitement when I was there as their patron, Derek Nimmo the actor, was visiting, but it was certainly a warm, happy and cheerful home, which is exactly what the Walkers intended.

Once again the BBC and my tape recorder had allowed me behind doors that might never have opened to me in normal circumstances or in places that might have simply escaped my attention. As it was I found Luppitt a unusual and fascinating village, which is where we started..

Lydford

Lydford is another special place amongst my choice of Devon villages, for two reasons. Firstly, as you will have read elsewhere in this book, my family holidays were spent in the West Country in the late '50's early '60's when it would take literally hours to drive from London to Devon.

After one of her 'clear outs' my mother sent me a whole batch of photographs, some of which record those days. These arrived just shortly after I had taken my young family to visit Lydford and the nearby Gorge. It was one of those glorious late autumn days, with the last of the leaves still on the trees, a clear blue sky and a certain crispness in the air and I can remember our picnic lunch that day, sitting outside in the unseasonable sunshine.

I can't however remember much of my visit to Lydford as a boy, although amongst the photographs that my mother had sent was one of me in short trousers standing in the woods with the spectacular White Lady waterfall in the background. Without any form of deliberate planning on my part, during our visit some thirty years later I took an identical photograph of our son, then aged seven, in exactly the same spot. Comparing the two pictures little has changed, the most striking thing being that the photograph of me is a faded black and white and the one of Ben is in colour. Perhaps the subconscious does play strange tricks and there are more things in heaven and earth than are dreamt of in our photography!

The author at Lydford Gorge as a boy.

The other reason for Lydford retaining a special place in my memory is that I was introduced to the village by a man called David Dunhill. David came to BBC Radio Devon as a voice tutor and essentially is best described as a gentleman of the 'old school'. Meticulous in both manner and dress, it was his job to travel the country visiting the local stations and try to coach would be broadcasters to use their voices in a relaxed and natural way, a skill in which he reigned supreme. On one visit to Radio Devon David and I were discussing what I did for the radio station and I told him about the Village Profile series.

"Have you ever been to Lydford?" he asked. Well of course the answer was yes, but not for the radio programme so within a few weeks and armed with my tape recorder I arrived in time to join David and the choir practicing in the pretty church of St Petrock. I wasn't allowed simply to record that session either. David thrust a hymn book into my hand and I was encouraged to join in, although I'm not sure that my voice added much to the quality of the choir that night.

John Arscott, St Petrock's church warden, explained that the church as it exists today – a squat, typical Dartmoor granite building with an immaculately kept churchyard – was preceded by a wooden structure. This had been burnt down by the Danes and then a stone church was built in its place. Over the years this orginal building was added to and grew to its present shape and size today. The pews, made of solid oak with carved ends, are decorated with fishes, animals and flowers and are quite beautiful but just inside the porch is what for me is one of the most unusual and interesting features of Lydford's church.

It's here that you find the tombstone of George Routledge, Watchmaker, and its inscription.

> 'Here lies in horizontal position
> The outsize case of
> GEORGE ROUTLEDGE, Watchmaker
> Whose abilties in that line were an honour
> To his profession.
> Integrity was the mainspring,
> And prudence the regulator
> Of all the actions of his life...
> So much regulated were all his motions
> That he never went wrong...'

A marvellously witty epitaph for a man who might otherwise have been forgotten after his death in 1802.

As well as its splendid church Lydford also has a castle, the remains of which can still be seen today. Originally an earth works built to supplement the natural defence of the gorge against attacks from the Danes the earth works were replaced by a stone built castle in Norman times and were used as a court and a prison by the Dartmoor tin miners. Norman Fry, who has lived in Lydford all his life, told me of the legend of the ghost of the black pig which is supposed to haunt the ruined keep. Rumour has it that this is Judge Jeffreys, of Bloody Assizes' fame, transformed into the shape of a pig and although there is no record of the infamous judge having stayed in Lydford it seems as good an explanation as any other. Norman is not too sure that the black pig's appearances aren't connected with the proximity of the castle to the Castle Inn next door and perhaps sightings are due to "an extra pint or two sometimes."

Every year about 50,000 people visit the village. Most come to see the Gorge of course but it would be a shame to miss the centre of the village which is very beautiful with its single main street lined with granite stone houses.

These houses are a far cry from the earliest dwellings in and around Lydford and its Gorge. At one time the sides of the Gorge, which contain a network of caves and cave entrances, used to provide shelter of sorts to bands of ferocious outlaws, bandits and robbers whose very appearance used to strike the fear of God into the more law abiding population. However, today's visitors need have no worries as the Gorge is safe in the hands of the National Trust.

There is still a hint of the evil and sinister about and anyone visiting Lydford Gorge must be certain to include the Devil's Cauldron, part of the ravine section. A spectacular and really quite frightening pool, some ten or twelve feet deep over which is suspended a plank, along which you can venture out and stand, if you dare, right above the crashing, foaming, boiling water.

At the other end of the Gorge is the White Lady Waterfall. It's some 40 to 50 minutes walk from the Cauldron, although there is another car park at this end of the gorge for those who prefer not to walk. The water cascades in a thin, sheer ribbon of white some ninety feet from the cliff above and when the river tributary is in full spate it's a majestic sight. For my money Lydford and the Gorge is best seen in the winter months or as I did with my family during the autumn. The village is less busy, the waterfall because of the autumn and winter rains is more breath-taking but if summer is the only time you can make it then I think so be it, just allow longer for the summer traffic and parking. Whatever time of year though, a visit to Lydford is a must. Thank you David Dunhill for enticing me back and I apologise for my singing!!

Lynmouth

Visiting Lynmouth today it's difficult to appreciate the events of 1952 which completely changed the face of this North Devon village. The scene that greets you at the bottom of the steep hill leading to Lynmouth is one of tranquil peace and calm far removed from the night of August 15th when after hours of continuous rain the rivers and water courses could no longer cope and mother nature unleashed its fury on the village. In compiling a Radio Village Profile of Lynmouth contemporary news reports from the village in 1952 from the BBC sound archives sent a shiver down my spine in their descriptions of the sheer devastation that came to this part of Devon's coast nearly forty years ago.

Lynmouth, along with Lynton its twin village which sits some 500 feet above Lynmouth, had a world wide reputation long before those tragic events in 1952. It was well known as a seaside resort and had developed from a place where people came to drink the sea water to somewhere with an international reputation thanks to the romantic poets, Wordsworth, Coleridge and Shelley who visited the area and helped to put it on the map.

Lynmouth was originally a small cluster of fishing cottages around a harbour, while Lynton was a farming village. In common with other fishing centres on this coast the herring shoals disappeared, the wool spinning industry of Lynton collapsed and economic depression set in. However, in 1800 a small hotel opened on the site of the Globe Inn which was followed some 7 years later by the opening of the first Valley of Rocks hotel and Lynmouth began the climb out from the depths of recession.

One of the first problems facing tourists wishing to visit the area was transport. The railway didn't arrive until 1898 and the moorland roads were very difficult but the industry grew because of the development of steamers on the Bristol Channel. Steamer travel was expensive so visitors arriving in the village often stayed all season, a far cry from the week or fortnight which makes up the holiday of today. With the exceptional scenery of the area, where Exmoor meets the sea in a rugged steep coastline, Lynmouth prospered.

Eric Delderfield, who lives in Devon, has written a book on the Lynmouth flood disaster and he got to the village just two days after the Lyn river changed its course and the torrent of water swept all before it completely changing the face of Lynton. The devastation was complete and the BBC reports, to which I referred earlier, talk of people's homes reduced to only one wall by tumbling rocks, resembling dolls' houses, with the doors open, with beds and bedding, tables, mirrors and kitchen dressers all being exposed to view. Eric told me of the sight that met his eyes when he arrived in Lynmouth. "It was an absolute hopeless mess. It looked much like the scenes that you saw in London during the Blitz." One of the most remarkable things about this episode in the history of Lynmouth was the speed with which the rescue services were on the scene. "It was quite incredible, wonderful. Within two days the army had moved in, the W.R.V.S. were there, the Police, everybody just piled in. As far as I know, and I was very close to the operation there was never any bickering between one group or organisation and another. It was absolutely fantastic."

The strange thing was that in the midst of a scene that as Eric said echoed war time demolition there were little pockets and things in the

Lynmouth after the flood.

village that had escaped damage. Eric Delderfield remembers "that in one hotel three of the walls had gone and there was only one wall left standing. On this wall was a mantlepiece on which objects still stood and by the side of that on a table there was a dish containing a dozen eggs and not one of them was broken." Another story that Eric recalled was that of "two old ladies who lived up Watersmeet Road. They had gone to bed, slept right through and the first that they knew of the flood was when they looked out next morning."

Aside from the terrible physical damage to the village, thirty four people died and even after the waters subsided some were never traced. For me one of the photographs of the time which best conveys the extent of the disaster and the sheer power and force of the waters which hit the village on that night is of a car, one of many on the beach mangled almost beyond recognition, looking for all the world as if it had been blown up by a modern day land mine. It is difficult to conceive of the terror and havoc of that night and Lynmouth was never the same again.

Delderfield thinks, however, that the community spirit of Lymouth has completely recovered. "Within a year the spirit was back in spite of what happened. They're tough people in North Devon you know."

The village was largely rebuilt in the years that followed and the course of the river diverted so that the tragedy could not repeat itself and the tourists still come, many to hear of that August night but most to enjoy Lynmouth for what it is today, visit the dramatic Valley of the Rocks and wonder at the scenery.

The historical records of the R.N.L.I. also feature Lynmouth for an heroic rescue that took place in 1899, when the Lynmouth lifeboat had to be launched. Edward Nightingale, a former Mayor of Lynmouth, takes up the story. "There was an S.O.S. from a ship in Porlock Bay and the weather was too bad to launch the lifeboat in Lynmouth, which at the time was a rowing boat or 'puller'. The decision was taken to haul the boat on its carriage some nine miles overland, up Countisbury Hill and down Porlock Hill the other side." One only has to visit the village to understand why this launch has become one of the epic stories of the R.N.L.I.

No visit to the area would be complete without a ride on the famous Lynmouth/Lynton cliff railway which connects the two villages and affords a fabulous view of the re-shaped village and valley below. The railway works on a counter-balance principle down the one in one and three quarter gradient, with water being used to fill a reservoir on the railway cars so that the car at the top is heavier than the one at the bottom. The water in the bottom car is released making the top car travel downwards after the brakes are let off, pulling the bottom car up the cliff. The railway is nearly 100 years old and is open throughout most of the year, except for maintainance, and it is perhaps ironic that the water from the very river which so changed the village provides the motive power for Lynmouth's cliff railway on which so many thousands of visitors see a very different place to the village which existed pre-1952.

The storms of early 1990 have taken their toll on North Devon yet again and as I write this reports have come in on a land slip near Lynmouth's cliff railway reminding older residents of those dark days which they would rather forget – the power of Mother Nature can be terrible and man it seems is powerless against it.

Moretonhampstead

Moretonhampstead is known as the gateway to Dartmoor and when I went there I started my visit not on the moor but just outside the town at the farm of Arthur Harvey. Although Arthur primarily raises sheep on the farm, in a way he led the field in diversification – not in terms of the holiday accommodation and camping facilities there – but because of the shooting that he offers. And it's not game birds or clay pigeons that are the target because here, just outside the small village (or town as the locals would prefer you called it) Arthur runs a national shooting centre.

It all started when Arthur trained the British Olympic team for a gruelling cross country and marksmanship event in which competitors ski over a specified distance and then fire, either in a prone or a standing position, a fixed number of rounds at a target before setting off on the next leg. It makes great demands on those taking part. They have to race as fast as possible and then steady themselves for precision target shooting.

The hills and contours surrounding the farm provide the ideal training ground for the event and although Arthur cannot always promise snow to the would be team members he can simulate hard physical cross country conditions from which the man has to recover and then shoot accurately. In addition to the Olympic Team training Arthur teaches shooting to a 'range' of people from absolute beginners to experts firing weapons from air pistols and rifles to target 22's such as the Olympic team uses.

It had been many years since I did any target shooting at school and to say that I was a bit rusty when Arthur took me to the rifle range was an understatement. Under his expert instruction however I did at least manage to hit the target, although listeners to the radio were led to believe that I did better than I did in reality. Thankfully Arthur didn't spoil the illusion on tape!!

As with many of my Village Profile visits I found that the Chairman or Clerk to the local Parish Council was of great help in painting in some of the village background. George Friend, who has been Moretonhampstead's Clerk for the last twenty seven years was no exception. "It's an old market town," he told me, "although we don't have a market here now. That closed in 1927 and the market moved to Newton Abbot. Originally the town was known as Moreton meaning an enclosed settlement near the Moor and then in the fourteenth century the Earl of Hampstead from London who owned the land added the name Hampstead. So it was called Moretonhampstead and still is to this day."

Moreton is very centrally placed about twelve miles from Exeter, Okehampton, Princetown and Newton Abbot, the very gateway to Dartmoor. It's perhaps fitting then that Ian Mercer, Chief Executive of Dartmoor National Park, should live here. Dartmoor attracts over seven million visitors a year – which partly accounts for why Moreton gets so busy with summer traffic – and I asked Ian if he thought that the Moor was important to the town and its residents. "I think it's very important and the economy of the town, although it's very healthy in the winter, depends on the people that pass through the place in the summer for its surpluses. There's also a good resident tourist population as well. There's no question that a lot of visitors spend money in Moreton." There is also no question that they leave behind them tons of litter every year so if visiting please, pleads Ian, take your litter home with you. It's unsightly and also dangerous to the stock that roams the moor.

A view across Dartmoor near Moretonhampstead.

If you take the Postbridge Road out of the town you come across one of Moreton's most unusual, and certainly to my young daughter endearing features, the Miniature Pony Centre run by Tony and Jane Dennis. Tony is a former race jockey, with a build to match, a small slight wiry man, who with his wife has bred miniature ponies for the last twenty years. They had been breeding thoroughbred horses alongside the miniatures but found that they had so many visitors to the stables to look at the Shetlands without paying any charge, that they decided to expand the idea and start the Minature Pony Centre. They searched all over Devon for a suitable property, with good road access, and they found their present site which was only three miles from where their former stables had been.

There was a tremendous amount of work to do to create the tourist attraction as it is today – lakes had to be dug and filled, stabling and a restaurant built, car parking constructed but the end result is something of which the couple can feel justly proud and, judging from the excited grins on children's faces when they visit, it is a worthy addition to the Moretonhampstead area.

Back in the town I met David Baker who at one time had been Secretary to Devon's Young Farmers' Club but is now an organiser for the Duke of Edinburgh Award Scheme. He is also Co-Editor, along with Gary Cox of Moretonhampstead's own Community Newspaper with a circulation of over 350, all delivered by dedicated volunteers. Jill, David's wife, lends a hand too and when I went to their house the proof copy of an edition was just coming off the 'printing press' in their sitting room. A very practical way of residents keeping in touch with the town's news – the modern day word processed equivalent of the town crier.

As I had learned from George Friend, Moretonhampstead, has an ancient history and indeed has its own history society. Ken Theobald is a past Chairman of the Society and took me to St Andrews Church to show me round. An amusing sideline to this visit was that I couldn't understand why on the recorded interview with Ken I was getting 'feedback' on the test tape that I did and it took me a while to deduce that the problem was that Ken was wearing a hearing aid which created the interference. Having asked him to turn it down a bit he told me about two tomb stones in the porch way that commemorate the death of two French officers who were living in Moretonhampstead during the time of the Napoleonic Wars, having been released on parole from Dartmoor Prison. Inside the splendid church Ken told me more of the town's history.

"It was mainly a town where the wool trade, and serge making in particular were important. There were three mills here at one time, but there's only traces of one left now down at the bottom of Lime Street. But Moretonhampstead was the place where travellers would stop naturally because it was a sort of junction from North to South and East to West with people who didn't want to go over Dartmoor going round it. The movement of people going through meant that in the eighteen hundreds the town supported thirteen pubs. Today we've only five."

It seems that little changes really. Moretonhampstead is still as popular with travellers or visitors today as it was then as they pass through this gateway to Dartmoor.

Musbury

Musbury is about three miles in one direction from the well known carpet town of Axminster and the holiday resort coastal town of Seaton in the Eastern corner of Devon. There's a good mixture of both old and newer buildings in the village, the Post Office for example is over two hundred years old as is much of the village centre, but as you move to the outskirts of the village there's newer council houses and bungalows for more elderly people. With a population of just about five hundred the village has a hall, which has now been totally rebuilt at a cost of £45,000, a pub and a small school with about twenty five children on the roll when I was there.

Kathleen Coombs is what is rather grandly described as the village contact and I asked her to explain exactly what this meant. "People come to me if they want any help or advice. I hold a list of places where they can go, like solicitors, Citizens Advice Bureaux etc. I don't actually give advice myself, I just point them in the right direction, a point of contact." An idea that seemed very sensible to me and should be more widely taken up in other villages where often loneliness and isolation can set in un-noticed by neighbours.

Musbury's old Post Office.

Kathleen told me that loneliness in Musbury shouldn't really be a problem though because there are about ten different clubs and groups here and something to suit most tastes. Clem Crutchley, when we met described himself as a 'one man club', the founder and only member of 'The Retired Layabouts Club', Musbury branch.

"I don't get up to an awful lot now, although I was very active in the village but I've relinquished a lot of what I used to do due to advancing age, mainly on the principle that I think that younger people should take over because its their village as well and their future."

Musbury has a particular connection with one of Devon's most famous sons as Clem went on to tell me. "There's a big connection between the Drake family and Ash House on the outskirts of the village. I believe that the first Duke of Marlborough was born there and the legend, if you can call it that, carries on in that the house is called Drake's Hall, the village hall bears the name of Drake, and the village pub is The Golden Hind."

There's a splendid monument to Drake in Musbury Church which attracts people from great distances to come and see it. The memorial is actually dedicated to Francis Drake's brother, Barnard. The story has it that the two brothers didn't really get on terribly well together, and Barnard came up to this area of Devon to make his own way in life away from his brother who became one of England's most well known historical figures.

Musbury has its own castle, another real link with the past, although if you follow the directional sign to the castle you will be disappointed if you expect to see the crumbled ruins of some Norman grey stone walls. Musbury Castle is an earthworks or large hill which rises behind the church and orignally there would have been some kind of earthworks or fortification at the top.

In my travels around the villages of Devon I have often come across what I can only describe as 'real characters' and Archie Arnold in Musbury was certainly one of those and although he wouldn't really be drawn into talking much on tape he did tell me that in terms of work he "does as little as possible." Lawrence Littley was another character and indeed just prior to my visit Lawrence had become a figure of some notoriety, not only in the village and in the surrounding area, but nationally as well after his story was told in the Sun newspaper.

Lawrence described himself as a 'poor broken down dairy farmer' and it was in following his occupation that he hit the national news. Farmers collect the dung and straw from the yard when the cows are in during the winter and when ground conditions permit they spread this dung on the fields. Well this had been Lawrence's intention but "unfortunately I came down through the village with the dung spreader working and managed to spray quite a few houses and cars on the way through." Having gone in for a bit of redecoration in the village I wondered how the house and car owners had taken it . "They took it in a proper fashion, I must say. No-one, no-one complained. No-one at all. My wife and I came out with a hose pipe to clean it all off, but people and the press got to hear about it and believe you me that was some fame that I could well do without."

Hilda Turl lived in Musbury as a child before moving away from the village, to return in later life. "I remember that my father kept cows and I used to deliver the milk around door to door with a pail and a measure. We used to have a blacksmith here, a shoe repairer and a butcher. My grandfather was the butcher here in the village and he used to deliver round in a horse and cart. We didn't have electricity of course, it was all oil lamps and old fashioned stoves. Do you know, when I look back I reckon life may have been harder but they were good old days." Hilda's face lit up at the memories as they came flooding back.

Archie Arnold had spent much of his life travelling the world and spent nineteen years in the army but reckons that there is nowhere to touch Musbury as a place to live. After the army he had come back to the village to live and tried it for twelve months but it was 'too quiet' so off he went and worked away for another sixteen years before he felt 'old age' coming on and returned – "It's a lovely place, you can't beat it."

Newton Ferrers

I was first introduced to Newton Ferrers by friends of ours who take their caravan there for the occasional weekend. Over one summer Bank Holiday, when the weather was unusually hot and the skies almost cloudless, my family and some other friends joined them. After a pub lunch waiting for the tide to turn, we set off in one of our friend's Mirror dinghy.

John, another friend who was staying in the area, was on a windsurfer. In spite of my protestations I was persuaded to climb aboard the dinghy. 'Steady about' soon changed to 'Ship ahoy' as we narrowly avoided other large and small craft in the Newton Ferrers creek.

John, cutting a dashing sight, as he tacked back and forth on his windsurfer – an art which is much more difficult than it looks – turned back; but we intrepid sea farers kept going, zig-zagging our way, somehow managing to avoid being mown down, and seemed to spend hours getting to the beach where we had arranged to meet the family only to find they had got fed up with the wait and long since returned to the village and the pub.

The day was particularly memorable because as the Mirror was launched I had been delegated to 'park' the boat trailer on the foreshore. I had been careful to check with the skipper that I had left it positioned correctly, so it was with more than a little concern that on our return the trailer was nowhere to be seen. The tide had come in and the trailer was now several feet under water! It was retrieved by John and myself with a certain degree of mirth and the Mirror strapped in place. Our day's sailing had ended with me thinking that there is more to this lark than meets the eye and that there WAS merit in the life of a landlubber.

We returned in time to catch some of the Newton Ferrers regatta and the whaler racing but more of that later. The day was a lesson in how deceptive wind and tides can be on this part of the coast and how extreme care is needed and how the sea and tidal waters should be treated with great respect. Another clear memory is of my young daughter, then about five, who decided that having all finally met up again at the pub she would fall of the quayside wall into the water. Able to swim she thought it all highly funny to start with until the cold set in. All in all it was an eventful first visit to Newton Ferrers.

The village is the picture post card ideal of what one imagines a small Devon resort to be. You arrive at the sea and the cottages along the river frontage down a narrow twisting hill and there suddenly is the water. Across the other side is Noss Mayo and there is a fierce rivalry between the two villages especially at regatta time. It's hard to believe that Newton, as it known locally, is so close to Plymouth, and in the winter it's a quiet almost deserted place but as with so much of Devon, it's a very different story in the summer, when the place is throbbing with visitors, like me, coming to enjoy both the scenery and the water. Orph Sheppard who has lived in the village all his life has seen the village change with this influx of "new people coming in and the older ones dying out" and although it doesn't cause real resentment there's a certain sadness in the village that so much of the property, especially the cottages down by the creek, is now owned by outsiders, a cry that I have heard often in my travels around the county.

When the tide is out you can walk across from one village to the other and when it's in you have to take the ferry boat. In 1924, Len Carter who was then aged four, moved to the village from Canada and since 1934 he was the man responsible for running the ferry. "Life used to revolve around fishing and families like the Fosters and the Hockadays who used to go out crabbing every day in their little boats. My father and I used to run the ferry but my youngest son runs it now. In our days it was rowing of course and that was hard work. You've got to watch the sea too because we can get something like the Severn bore coming up here. In 1947 I think it was there was a wave which came up which it was reckoned was about fifteen feet high". No wonder we had found it tough going in the Mirror dinghy!

The regatta is a big annual event and there are competetive rowing, swimming and sailing matches between the two villages which go on over a ten day period. Originally the races were staged using whaling boats borrowed from Plymouth dockyard but today the boats are made in the village and as Joan Turner told me "The regatta's a great thing" in the Newton Ferrers' calendar.

The Newton Ferrers Regatta.

In my travels around Devon I have met some marvellous characters and there have been few better than Edgar Foster who has lived in Newton Ferrers most of his life, although he claims duel nationality having spent twenty seven years in Noss Mayo. He must be quite unique in terms of the regatta having rowed for both sides at different times. "After I came over here" he said, "they used to throw stones at me from Noss side. Whether they resented me coming over I don't know. It could get pretty rough you know. I can remember that my father had a boat built for the regatta. It was 19 foot six long and with sails and a pair of paddles it cost £14." Times have certainly changed a bit. "In those days the boats had no centre boards and it was all sailing. If there was no wind you had to row of course. I learnt to skull a boat, that's one paddle over the stern in Noss Creek and fell overboard before ever I went to school. It's quite an art and those that can do it will tell you what belongs to it. It's quite a strenuous business you know. It's good for your figure too because it tries your tummy muscles!"

As I visited Newton Ferrers for the Village Profile series it was more than appropriate for Edgar to recount what for me remains one of the best radio stories that I have heard and I retell it now in his own words.

"There was a lady who used to live over at Noss called Mrs Simms and I used to go there and help the old man in the garden a bit. She used to give me a slice of seed cake and a jug of cocoa but anyway, along comes radio. At first it was cats' whiskers and then it gradually got to valve sets and they were wonderful. I was passing the house one day and the old lady says to me, 'Edgar you come in here a minute. I've got something for you to listen to.' So I went into the kitchen and she had one of these valve sets and there was a man broadcasting on it. I'm not sure what he was talking about, maybe it was the news I'm not sure. But anyway, she said to me 'Now then Edgar. that man's up to London! And do you know if you shut the window, you can still hear him!'".

The wonders of the modern world. One thing is certain, that Edgar and the 'old guard' of somewhere like Newton Ferrers will never properly be replaced and not only is Newton Ferrers a delightful place to visit but meeting Edgar, hearing him spin his yarns in his lazy Devon drawl was a real pleasure. The seafood pub lunch was good too!

Otterton

Every so often in researching or approaching the making of a radio programme, or feature, the way of painting a living picture in sound becomes crystal clear. At other times you have to struggle to find a way of doing it, adding light and shade and holding the listeners in a shifting and interesting sound pattern or series of location effects. Otterton was an example of the first, when on visiting the mill and discovering that it was still worked and the wheel still turned to grind flour, my path was clear. Hence the Village Profile largely centred on the mill, with the wheel turning, corn being ground whilst I talked to the mill owner about the process of milling, but more of that later.

Otterton is situated in the valley of the River Otter in East Devon and much of the land surrounding the village is owned by Lord Clinton whose family run and control the Clinton Devon estates. Richard Waller is Lord Clinton's Land Agent and he manages the estate on which there are many tenanted farms. The estate also runs three dairy farms of its own. Forestry too figures largely in the work on the estate and has long been an interest of Lord Clinton and his family before him.

With such a large estate in the area it doesn't seem very surprising to find just a mile or so out of the village one of Devon's foremost agricultural centres, Bicton College. Malcolm Flourey is the principal at Bicton and in front of the main college building, a fine Georgian construction with wonderful views across the parklands and towards Bicton Park and its lake, I asked Malcolm to tell me more about the college. "The college itself is one of about 39 national County Colleges. As well as the farm here at Bicton in East Devon we have also taken on another farm at Merton in North Devon where we can learn farming under different soil and climatic conditions than here. At Bicton we probably have to farm in a more diversified way than you would on a typical Devon farm in this part of the county, but we have to do that to meet the needs of the students. We have a large herd of dairy cows, an indoor pig unit being built up alongside an outdoor pig breeding unit as well as beef, sheep and poultry units. Half the land is planted to grass, the rest to winter cereals, potatoes and a variety of other crops."

"At the moment we have some two hundred full time students as well as a very large number of short course and part time students and we also do work with schools and Youth Training. It's really a College of the Countryside with a staff of about one hundred and sixty."

Across the lake from the agricultural college there is Bicton Park, which I mentioned earlier. Bicton Park is a tourist spot which used to promote itself as providing the ideal 'Family Day Out.' There's a woodland railway which runs around the lakeside, a museum of transport and agricultural machinery and effects, a children's adverture play area with mini go karts but most impressive are the gardens which are beautifully laid out and kept and a source of great pride to Tom Robinson, the General Manager and his staff. I remember going there one summer and seeing a demonstration of hawk flying which was immensely impressive. Just next door is Bicton Arena, a showing jumping venue which attracts many of the big names in the business during the competitive season.

In Otterton, I met Michael Harrison who had written a book on the village. "I didn't call it a village history because I didn't want to make it too precise. I wanted to tell the story of Otterton really, not put people off as I wanted to try and sell the booklet and precise dates and things like that tend to bore people. I wanted to make it a bit more interesting. Until about twenty years ago, the whole village to all intents and purposes was owned by the Clinton Devon Estates. Not only the land but every single house in it. Most people were working on the estates but as agriculture changed, and changed so rapidly,so there was less and less work on the land and it changed from being a population of leaseholders to being a population of freeholders with no real connection to the village."

One of the most surprising things that Michael discovered during his research for the book was the volume of cider that was produced in the village. "According to the old maps there were about thirty six acres of cider orchards around the village which produced a great number of hogsheads, some of which was for home consumption and the rest was sold."

I moved from Michael's house to the mill, or rather opposite the mill itself, the home of Desna Greenhow, who also owns and runs Otterton Mill. Yes, the village miller is a woman and one of only a handful of women in the trade in the country. Before getting the enormous mill wheel turning she has to open a sluice gate allowing the mill leat or stream to change course and run crashing and foaming towards the wheel which provides the mill with its power.

Desna describes the mill as working using one thousand year old technology, which is as good a description as any I could think of. By opening gates and allowing the water to flow through the channel in which the giant water wheel sits suspended, the paddles catch the flow of water and begin to turn the wheel itself. As the wheel picks up speed, then a series of gears are engaged for it to start operating the grinding machinery and the milling process can begin. The mill stones, which to begin with are set apart from each other and weigh a ton and a half and measure four feet across, are then moved closer together until they are the right distance apart to begin grinding. The skill of the miller lays in getting the distance between the stones right because not only does this determine the fineness of the resulting ground flour, but should they get too close and touch, sparks would literally fly and could cause an explosion as the flour dust ignites.

Desna Greenhow at work at Otterton Mill.

I had every confidence in Desna's skill and ability though and stood watching her as she went about getting the mill going, something that visitors to Otterton can see for themselves.

"We produce about three quarters of a ton of flour a week," she told me, "which doesn't sound a lot, although it is by domestic standards and a lot of it is used in the little bakery which we have here."

I can well remember that Desna was kind enough to give me a loaf of Otterton Mill bread before I left, a kind of nutty brown whole meal affair, and before driving back to the studios I sat in my car tearing off big crusty chunks, leaving very little to take home to my wife and family so delicious was it.

Otterton is a little bit tucked away off the beaten track but in the village itself I was lucky to have watched what must be a dying art demonstrated by Desna at the mill. As a family we have enjoyed visits to both Bicton Park and the Arena and I have little doubt that at the College they are equipping youngsters of today with the knowledge and skills to face the challenge of modern farming in all its guises and almost as much in terms of variety as is offered by the village of Otterton itself.

Payhembury

When I visited Payhembury with my tape recorder and the subsequent programme was broadcast, it provoked a lady who lived in the Parish to write a letter of complaint to the Manager of the Radio station. She was then, I think, Parish Clerk and she complained that the picture that I had 'painted in sound' gave the impression of this East Devon village, a few miles from the bustling market town of Honiton, living in the past, inhabited only by the old with little going on to either interest or involve young people. Perhaps at the time this was a justifiable complaint, because it was certainly the older residents of Payhembury who had captured my interest.

I make no apology therefore for focusing on one of these older Payhembury people here, although I accept that there is a vibrant village school in the village, a football club, a swimming club, cricket seems to be undergoing a revival etc etc but to me the man that I met several years ago now typifies much of the spirit of rural Devon that I have tried to capture in these pages.

Cyril Warren is dead now but I can very vividly recall his tall, slightly stooped, willowy frame clad in a long brown coat, brown trilby hat on head, long walking stick in one hand with shopping basket over his other arm making his way from his farm, Cokesputt, into the village. Cyril had for many years carried on driving, but with failing eyesight saw the good sense in leaving his old grey Wolsey at home rather than continue to terrify those on his route to the post office, garage or village shop, who had sometimes to move smartly out of his way as they saw him coming towards them his face almost pressed against the windscreen to see where he was going.

Cyril's family had lived in Cokesputt – its name derived from Cock Pit, where the village cock fighting used to take place – for about 200 years, and I remember going to visit him at the house which stands back from the road into the village. It's a proud looking house, with a verandah along the front clad in wysteria. Inside it was rather dark, due no doubt to the creeper cutting out the daylight and Cyril asked me into his kitchen. It seemed that much of the rest of the house was uninhabitable with rooms having fallen into disrepair, Cyril moving as they did so and his living space becoming more restricted inside this vast old Devon farmhouse.

I can also remember his concern for his cat, perhaps because it was his only real companion, which had a bad eye infection and which the vet was advising should be put down. In a vast tome, which charted the history of the county of Devonshire, he showed me a picutre of his house in his Grandfather's time and one could see what a gentleman's mansion it had been in its glory.

Cyril was born in Payhembury and could well remember the village wheelwrights, the thatcher, harness maker and the baker. As a farmer he told me of going to market by pony and trap, the passing of the horse on the farm and the arrival of the pneumatic tyre and the tractor. He also told me about the blanket club in the village which his grandmother ran. The elderly in the village could 'rent' extra blankets for the winter and there was also a boot club to help the younger members of the community as well as several other village charities, including the distribution of a piece of beef at Christmas time.

Payhembury Christmas Club with Cyril Warren as a young man.

He had seen the village grow and expand and many changes in farming, from the price of finished pigs to mechanisation. But through it all he seemed to have retained a degree of peace and above all dignity, perhaps because of his life long association with the church – he was a Church Warden and played the organ for over fifty years before his poor eyesight forced him to give that up as well.

Perhaps this left him little to live for. Perhaps Cyril saw the changes that were just around the corner or perhaps it was simply that his time had come, whatever happened Cyril Warren died. It is at this point of the story that I should declare an interest for I was only able to follow the sequel to Cyril's death as my wife and myself live just outside Payhembury.

The changes in village life that Cyril had spoken of are to me perhaps best typified by the village centre where true enough you

111

find the traditional village green, a traingle opposite the pub, The Six Bells, the lovely church set back on one side next to the war memorial and a row of thatched, white cob walled houses. But further along from the church you found not only the school opposite Capels' garage and Post Office but also the Leachs' mill. Right in the heart of the village a huge corrugated roofed monster of a building which spewed out fine dust and the smell of animal feed processing over the whole vicinity. A fine example of the new sitting most unhappily with the old. Add to this the giant lorries delivering and collecting from the mill premises via the vast weighbridge and you have some idea of the impact and the danger which existed.

The mill is now closed down but the Leach farming business has expanded in all directions around the village.

After Cyril's funeral, which was well attended by many people of all ages, there was some long delay before the trustees of his estate put up the house and the farm in various parcels of land for sale. At the funeral, the Vicar had spoken of Cyril's love of the land and his good husbandry and as the auction of Cyril's estate drew near, there were many in the village who feared that one farmer in particular would outbid everybody else and buy the land – Mr Leach, the mill owner.

He already farmed several hundred acres around the village in what current day politicians might describe as 'an environmentally insensitive way'.

Hedges had been ripped out wholesale and virtually disappeared, the landscape was devoid of trees and there had been many complaints from people living in the village about the smell when he spread slurry from his extensive pig unit onto his fields.

There was intense interest in both the house and the land at the auction and eventually after the house sold for over £300,000 the various lots of land were indeed 'knocked down' to the Leachs. What has since followed I suppose must be regarded as inevitable but given that as I write this we have just had British Food and Farming Year, a national showcase for farmers to demonstrate how food production can work hand in hand with sensitivity to conservation, I and many others have been greatly upset to see monster earth moving machinery come onto what was once Cyril's land, Devon hedges disappear and the face of the countryside change overnight.

Leach would I'm sure argue that he has done it all in the name of intensive commercial farming. But I can't square that with the saying that we 'borrow the countryside from our children'. It's certain that after he has finished it will look nothing like it did when Cyril died. I'm not against progress. Changes come and others will follow but it seems an absurd situation when planners take such a tough line on building within the green belt but are toothless in the face of the devastation that some farmers create in the name of progress.

It's very sad and to my mind totally unnecessary. Before the auction of Cocksputt, which had always been my wife's dream house, we went to look at the property. There hanging in the dairy outbuilding was Cyril's long brown coat. A ghost of the former occupier. I seriously wonder if he's turning in his grave and what Mr Leach's grandchildren will make of what he has left them. The Payhembury of today, and the land around Cokesputt, is very different to the village and Parish that Cyril knew.

Princetown and Dartmoor Prison

PARCERE SVBJECTIS

Even those who have never visited Devon have a preconceived image of Dartmoor and its notorious prison at Princetown. The mental picture most often conjured up is perhaps culled from Conan Doyle's Sherlock Holmes' mystery "The Hound of the Baskervilles" – a bleak landscape of damp swirling mists, of desolate and deserted mooorland of a place best left to the elements, moorland sheep and ponies.

To an extent that picture can be confirmed by a visit to Princetown. We once had an American student staying with us and took her to see the famous prison on the Moor on a damp, still day in autumn. The prison was totally invisible, completely shrouded in mist. In any event, even on a fine day the visitor can only stare at the high walls which surround Dartmoor Prison, built by Napoleonic prisoners of war, having little idea of what lies beyond the walls designed to keep certain members of society apart from the rest of us.

Once again it was the magic words "BBC Radio" that gave me access and a glimpse of life behind the bars and the huge entrance gates, part of life in Princetown that very few visitors see, unless as 'guests' of Her Majesty or members of the Prison staff. The massive grey granite archway leads into the prison gatehouse, thence into the prison itself. In layout the prison is like a clock face with the gate at six o'clock. The nearest buldings to the gatehouse contain the offices, workshops and hospital and across the open yard the cell blocks, or wings of the prison radiate out like spokes of a wheel. The whole is surrounded by the imposing walls, topped with barbed wire.

There's a feeling of great space within the walls, but on the day of my visit, a keen January day with snow in the air, the wind gusting across the yard made me wish for one of the greatcoats that the prison officers wore. Today Dartmoor holds over 600 prisoners and perhaps uniquely each man has his own cell. There's a staff of about 300 to look after the category B inmates – people who in the main are serving long sentences, including some people sentenced to life. Every day about 100 of the prisoners leave the prison to work on the farm – which supplies the prison's needs – the forestry plantations and the quarry. For those left inside during the day there are workshops where a variety of tasks are undertaken from the sewing of mail bags to the making of metal barred gates for other prisons in the country and there's also work in the kitchens to assist in the task of preparing and cooking the food for the prison population.

Perhaps not unnaturally everywhere you go within the prison you need a prison officer to accompany you with a set of keys to unlock the giant metal doors to allow you to progress on a tour of Dartmoor. Within each workshop the scene is much the same as you might find on the outside although it was explained to me by the staff that the tools being used are very carefully monitored and checked. They can't afford for any to go missing! In addition to the workshops, prisoners can avail themselves of the full time education facilities at

Dartmoor and in their highly sophisticated computer section prisoners actually write many programmes used by schools across the county.

The wings of the prison come as no surprise really. Television images are confirmed. The walls are cream and grey painted brick, with the 4 landings or floors being connected by a central iron staircase. I did question the netting which runs above head height on ground floor level, until it was explained that this was to prevent things being thrown onto those below or to cater for potential suicide attempts.

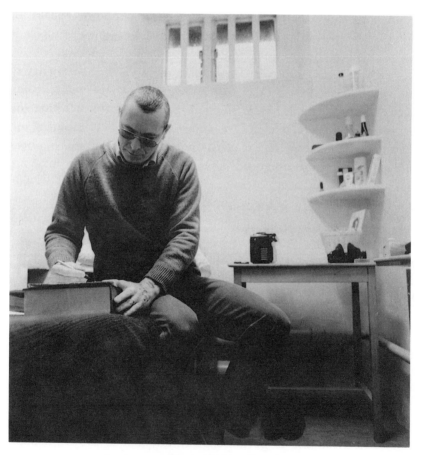

A prisoner on G wing in his cell at Dartmoor.

The cells lead off the landings on either side and although I didn't discover what he was in prison for – I wasn't allowed to ask – I was shown a cell by John, an inmate. This was a revelation and it was difficult to imagine being 'banged up' in what he described as his home, essentially a box room about 10 foot long by eight feet wide by the same high. The double barred window, at the opposite end to the cell door, is set high in the wall and can be slid open to provide some ventilation . The cell is basically furnished with a bed, table and locker and John explained that prisoners try to make their cells as 'hospitable as possible' decorating the walls with page three pin ups and so on because some can spend up to seventeen or eighteen hours a day locked in their cells if they don't have a job within the prison. "It can be very, very lonely" he said, "you've just got to try and keep yourself occupied with cell hobbies" – John played the guitar – and I could easily imagine the isolation that imprisonment might cause.

I was interested to discover that radios are allowed and John, like all others prisoners, has to go through the ritual of slopping out the bucket that he uses as a toilet in the cell every time he is unlocked, before meal times, exercise periods and association – times when prisoners are allowed to mix with each other.

Dartmoor Prison.

Although the cell was warm, as I said the outside weather was bitter, it was the ' slopping out 'that brought home to me the total infringement of a person's privacy that prison brings with it, although it is difficult to see how the regime at Dartmoor could be operated differently. Mike, a lifer 'on the Moor', told me that the regime could be very hard at times – "I think that after doing a long time it makes you introspective. I've been hot tempered, but since coming to Dartmoor I've become a Christian and am a very different person to the one that came here eleven years ago." Eleven years! For many people outside that in itself would represent a lifetime – my young son is just eleven. What then is Dartmoor, and indeed other prisons in the country, trying to achieve? Is it simply a matter of containment or is there an element of rehabilitation in serving a prison sentence? John May, the Governor at Dartmoor when I visited told me "Clearly we have a prime duty to the community at large to contain people and hold them securely. But over and above that what we try to do is find ways and means of offering everybody some kind of help so that when they go out of here they are a bit better equipped to cope with the problems of everyday life than when they came in."

Certainly it was my impression on my visit to the prison, that the staff try hard to run Dartmoor with both compassion and humour and I'm sure that there are times when a sense of humour is vital. This sort of warmth is not at all apparent from the outside of the prison of course but at the end of the day I, in common with the staff that work in shifts around the clock to keep the big ship that is Dartmoor on course twenty four hours a day, seven days a week, was able to walk out through the enormous gates, a free man and it's not all of Dartmoor's population that has the choice!

Spreyton

Tom Pearse, Tom Pearse, lend me your grey mare,
All along, down along, out along, leigh,
For I want to go to Widecombe Fair,
All along, down along, out along, leigh.
With Bill Brewer, Jan Stewer, Peter Davey, Peter Gurney,
Daniel Whiddon, Harry Hawk, Old Uncle Tom Cobley and All,
Old Uncle Tom Cobley and All.

Listeners to the Profile of Spreyton might well have been forgiven for thinking, as they heard Charlie Hill's beautiful, unaccompanied voice introduce the programme, that we had arrived in the wrong Devon village and that the presenter should have said 'We join Chris Smith today in the village of Widecombe.' But there is a very strong connection between Spreyton and Widecombe, which is featured later in this book.

The village is quite small with a population of around 300, half way betwen Crediton and Okehampton, names both familiar to the visitor to Devon, although Spreyton is a name that they probably won't know. For a village the size of Spreyton there are a surprising number of clubs, groups and associations and even a school which when I was there showed signs of quite rapid growth in numbers of children on the roll.

There's a touch of Christmas in the air all year round in Spreyton and John Anderton is continually counting the number of shopping days left as he runs a Christmas food hamper business which is based in the village. Employing over 20 people the business has been going for nearly 25 years and to an extent has provided employment opportunities which have grown as agricultural jobs have diminished due to farm mechanisation, although the jobs are largely filled by women. When the firm started, John injected £60 to float the business, today it's a multi-million pound business exporting to over 100 countries world wide. He also runs a farm holiday company with over 600 farms nationwide offering holiday accommodation, largely to overseas visitors.

Although farming has contracted as a source of employment, it is still important locally with dairy farming being the most popular and probably the most lucrative, although there are some mixed farms in the area with sheep and beef stock. Those with larger farms do employ a few people, like Charlie Hill did, but most are family firms and fairly self contained.

Charlie as well as running his 300 acre farm is also a devout collector of folk songs and liked nothing better than the opportunity to close his eyes, screw up his face in concentration and 'give you a song'. His solo voice trembled with emotion and there can be few better and more direct ways of story telling than the folk song and as we had heard at the start of the programme the famous Widecombe Fair song is such an example. Sadly I met Charlie quite recently in researching another book. He's now retired and lives in Drews-teignton but when I last saw him he was wracked with flu and a chest cold and his fine singing voice was starting to desert him and I feel myself lucky that I was able to met Charlie when he was still in his prime and capture forever on tape his wonderful voice.

Thomas Cobley Gent's tombstone.

So what's the connection between the tiny village of Spreyton and the world famous moorland village of Widecombe? The clue lies in the song that Charlie Hill had given at the start of the programme and in the name of the village pub in Spreyton. The Tom Cobley. Opposite the church porch there's a gravestone which bears the inscription 'Thomas Cobley Gent'. Now Widecombe claim that the Tom Cobley of the story lays buried in their village, although it's not certain that the Uncle Tom Cobley of the song did actually come from Widecombe. Today of course when Widecombe Fair is held in September, people come from miles around to attend and it's possible that it was Thomas Cobley Gent, now buried here, from Spreyton who borrowed Tom Pearse's grey mare and along with his friends made the trip to the fair with such tragic consequences and although there are no reports of the ghost of the horse, Tom Cobley or any of those named in the Widecombe Fair song being seen in Spreyton to 'haunt' those that live there today, in a sense his ghost lives on and there does seem to be a very strong connection between the two villages.

As well as the Thomas Cobley gravestone. the church is well worth a visit for the splendid avenue of lime trees planted in 1802. If the lime trees have been there for nearly two hundred years many other aspects of village life have changed. The village used to have their own wheel wright, who also installed a small generator to supply electricity to the chapel here. He's gone now along with the two village blacksmiths, the baker who used to deliver with a pony and trap, the saw mills and the shop which sold everything from sweets to petrol in two gallon cans.

Bill Daymond, who became a regular voice on the Radio Devon 'phone in programmes like 'Afternoon Sou'West' had been very helpful in arranging for me to meet people in Spreyton to talk to them for the programme about their village. Bill was a devoted listener to BBC Radio Devon and was in the 'communication' business himself. Having only recently moved to Spreyton from Chagford, he called it 'Chagiford', he ran a magazine for the disabled called 'The Orange Box'. Being disabled himself he knew well the challenge facing the physically handicapped and how important it was to keep in touch with what is going on.

Whatever the truth about Tom Cobley, standing amongst the row of lime trees in the church yard, as the wind rustled the leaves, it was easy to give credence to the Widecombe connection with the tiny village of Spreyton and let the imagination run wild...

And all the night long there was skirlings and groans
All along, down along, out along, leigh,
Tom Pearse's old mare and a rattling of bones
With Bill Brewer, Jan Stewer, Peter Gurney, Peter Davey,
Daniel Whiddon, Harry Hawk, Old Uncle Tom Cobley and All,
Old Uncle Tom Cobley and All.

That's Spreyton, the burial place of 'Thomas Cobley Gent.'

Swimbridge

Aside from contacting the Parish Council for local information another source of village wisdom and detail is the village Post Office, which was where I started my Profile of Swimbridge. The village is about four and a half miles from Barnstaple and as I discovered it has a big claim to fame far beyond the county borders, but more of that later.

Mrs Balment, the Post Mistress, told me that Swimbridge is well catered for with a regular bus and train service, village store, a butcher's shop, thriving primary school, – where I went to join the children for lunch – a lively church, a Methodist and a Baptist Chapel, village hall and the pub, the Jack Russell, named after a former rector.

There used to be a tannery in Swimbridge, which is now closed, and like many other Devon parishes farming is important locally with small family farms being passed down from generation to generation, although the farms no longer employ the numbers that they used to. At the time I visited, Mrs Balment told me that the residents were looking forward to the opening of the 'link road' which would take away some of the noisy traffic from the village and the main route through from South Molton to Barnstaple and make it much quieter, not that it would become 'dead' because as Mrs Balment told me there are many societies and groups in the village and that it was a lively place with something 'going on' most nights to suit all tastes.

Owen Dowling was one that I met who shared Mrs Balment's attitude towards the proposed new road. He's lived in the village for over 70 years. "We had several casualties on the road, the old A361, and we're looking forward to the new road being built. At the moment it can be dangerous for the school children. The school has been here since 1856 and a few years ago we got a footpath built which has made it better but once we have the new road, I know that parents will feel a lot more confident about their children going to the school from a safety point of view. When I was a boy, on the way to school, we used to play marbles in the road. You'd never get interrupted 'cos the traffic in those days was mainly horses and carts but today that would be impossible."

When I was in Swimbridge it was on the actual day that the Public Enquiry opened in South Molton on which route the new road should follow. Some six years later the road is open and life in Swimbridge has greatly improved. The arrival of the road is not all that has changed in the village. In the Post Office I saw a photograph which showed Swimbridge with mainly thatched houses, whereas today there's little thatch to be seen. Owen can also remember that up until 1951, villagers used to collect their water from stand pipes in the street but with a new mains system that was put in they have disappeared too, making life easier.

In 1937, Owen told me that he could remember the Bideford Electric Light Company bringing 'electric' to Swimbridge and it cost people a shilling a week. "I didn't have it right away though because I found that paraffin was cheaper to burn than electricity and seeing that wages were so low we had to watch the pennies."

Following a visit to the local playgroup, which was held in the old school room and run by Gillian Farrell and had been going for just over a year, I met David Netherway who told me more about Jack Russell, after whom the famous terrier dog was named. "He was the vicar of Swimbridge from 1883 and he stayed here for 48 years. He bred the dog here and now its name and the name of the village is

The Rev.
John (Jack) Russell.

known throughout the world. In 1983, a hundred years after his death, we held a celebration in the village to commemorate Jack Russell and his dog with all sorts of events including a big terrier show and he's remembered to this day in Swimbridge. He is buried behind the church here, a church that I think is one of the most beautiful in North Devon, and there's a memorial window which the villagers installed to remember him."

The window in the Lady Chapel shows the Ascension with an inscription below 'To the glory of God and in the memory of John Russell (Jack was a nickname) for forty eight years vicar of the Parish buried on Ascension Day 1883, aged 87.' So his name lives on not only through the lovely memorial window but through the small wiry terrier dog which he bred and which became world famous.

At one time, Swimbridge was well known in Devon not only for the Jack Rusell terrier but also for its beer, Swimbridge Ales. Geoff Patten was the man behind the beer and in the programme he told me more. "We had two beers, Swimbridge Bitter and then we introduced a stronger beer called Devon Giant." But the brewery closed a few years ago because as Geoff told me "Really we couldn't get enough customers. We used to work here in the village, in the old tannery building. There was another employee besides myself and during the busy period we used to employ casual labour as well. The basic problem with starting your own brewery is that all the pubs which sell a lot of beer are tied to a brewery and it's difficult to get in and although we had quite a few customers, together they weren't selling sufficient beer to keep the brewery going."

A sad note on which to end and although the 'tied house' situation hasn't changed a great deal with the increased interest now in 'real beer' I wonder if perhaps Swimbridge Ales were a little ahead of their time and if the story might have been different in the 1990's. Who knows?

What is certain is that now the North Devon link road is open, in spite of the debate about which route it should follow, life in Swimbridge is very different from when I visited and perhaps if he were to come back today, Jack Russell might better recognise the village that he knew and loved for so long.

Tetcott

When I selected Tetcott, the border of Devon and Cornwall, I never envisaged that I would be starting the radio programme with the sound of a barking dog and a hissing goose, nor that the goose would have the rather smart name of Freeman. In fact barking dogs featured quite heavily in the Profile of Tetcott, but let me explain.

I first went to visit Sir Arscott Molesworth St Aubyn at Tetcott Manor and it was here that I ran into, almost literally, his dog and the goose that were guarding the manor house. In Sir Arscott's oak beamed, granite floored day room in the grand old house, I asked him about the size of the estate. "My father handed the estate over to my on my twenty first birthday and I've now run it for forty years. When I inherited it, it was about 5,600 acres and had 34 different holdings on it. I've sold some boundary farms so as to pay for modern farm buildings on the remaining farms which are all mainly dairy."

I asked him next about being 'Lord of the Manor', was it a role that he enjoyed? For me it conjured up a rather vague picture of someone rather remote riding around their estate on horseback with tenant farmers bowing and scraping as they passed by. "I don't like the phrase 'Lord of the Manor' and I don't like the word 'Squire' either. I didn't buy this land, although it has been in my family for generations and some of my tenants are fifth generation now. The thing that we all have in common is that we all feel that it is part of our job to leave the land in a better condition than when we took it."

I'll go along with that and there is certainly a great deal of wonderful countryside around the village and Tetcott Manor which is very well worth preserving. In the Parkland, or the Wilderness as it's known locally, I met Frank Moss and as we paused before going into the church, looking around the beauty of the area was almost breathtaking.

Holy Cross Church is quite a simple, almost starkly plain church and it was this that made it so striking. Frank, as one of the church wardens was keen to show me some of the pew ends which date back for centuries along with the list of rectors of Holy Cross which is hung on the church wall and starts in 1310. Today though, in common with many rural parishes, the vicar of Tetcott has another four parishes in his 'flock.' But Tetcott only has a small population with just about one hundred and fifty being on the electoral roll.

Brian Jennings was Chairman of the Tetcott Parish Council and he explained that the River Tamar borders the village and forms a boundary on the western edge of the parish. It was hardly surprising to learn therefore that there is a fishing club in Tetcott which takes full advantage of its position near the river. Aside from fishing, the village has a skittle club, there's a small village hall and even a Post Office and shop and although as Brian said "It's a very small community everybody enjoys living here, getting together and having fun and that's what life is all about."

Employment locally is either in agriculture, although there is Terry Rook who took the plunge into self employment and now runs a garage which is well supported by the village, or people have to travel to nearby Holsworthy to find work. When I was there Brian also told me about "having a fairly vibrant community here and it saddens everyone younger people having to move away to find housing", and his hopes that a solution to this particular problem was just around the corner. He, along with the Parish Council, had been pushing for a Housing Association to come into the village and build 'starter homes' which would be reserved for people with connections with Tetcott or first time buyers in the area. Building of these new homes was, Brian hoped, due to start in the year following my visit.

Dennis Downing with the South Tetcott Hunt.

You will have gathered that during the course of recording these village programmes for Radio Devon, my tape recorder has 'unlocked' the door to several obscure and different places which might not normally be 'open' to everybody. One of these was the dog kennels at Tetcott, where I met Dennis Downing who is Tetcott's professional huntsman with the South Tetcott Hunt.

"I look after the hounds in the kennels and on hunting days take them out to hunt." I got very confused when I asked Dennis how many hounds he was looking after as he replied "I've got twenty seven and a half couples of old hounds and they're just coming in from walk with the puppies which means there are eleven and a half couple of puppies coming in." When I asked him how many this made, both he and I got very confused – "I can only count in couples" he replied and as maths was never my strong point we gave up on this question and just decribed the pack as being quite large!

"We hunt up to twenty miles away, as far as Okehampton and the Hatherleigh area and also down to the sea at Crackington Haven."

I asked Dennis if the Fox Hound was a difficult dog to control and look after. "No not really. You get one or two that may be difficult, but on the whole they're quite docile and easy to handle. To start with a young puppy will go out to walk on the farms, which means that they go from the kennels to be looked after by a farmer or a hunt supporter before coming back into the kennels at nine or ten months and then they learn kennel discipline. Then when they first go out they are collared up to an old hound and they will pick up the way of things from the old hound who teaches the young hound. You can't teach a hound to hunt though, he's bred to do that, but you can teach him other things like getting out of the way of car or a horse for instance."

What about the anti blood sport lobby and hunt protestors? Because there are times when things can get very unpleasent with demonstrators very passionately opposed to what Dennis and followers of the Tetcott Hunt are doing. "I think that most people who oppose hunting, don't live in the countryside or if they do they have come to live in it from the towns.If there was no hunting foxes would be persecuted. They'd be shot and wired and gassed. In a way it helps to preserve our landscape and countryside as well by leaving the covers where you might find a fox or a pheasent without grubbing them out, like they have done in the Midlands where farming is big business. The whole of the countryside would just be a plain of arable farming. It's the sporting heritage of this country that has helped shape the landscape of today."

However well reasoned that argument,I'm afraid that Dennis and hunting will always find opponents,but as little has changed in the Parish and village of Tetcott for years I'm sure that the hunt will remain for some years to come, alongside the Manor House still guarded no doubt by Freeman the Goose!

Uffculme

What a delightfully evocative name for a village, Uffculme. It's near Cullompton in Mid (or is it East?) Devon, in a sort of hinterland, not quite in the 'rich' east of the county nor laying exactly in the more secret quiet of mid Devon, it simply sits somewhere between the two. Uffculme is not an easy place to miss though, dominated as it is by the huge chimney stack of the old woolen mill, Coldharbour, just on the outskirts of the village.

A mill has probably existed here at Uffculme since at least the early eighteenth century, although the Doomsday Book suggests that a mill was sited here even earlier than this. During the first part of the 1700's it was a paper mill but was almost completely destroyed in great floods part way through the century and in 1753 was rebuilt as a mill for grinding corn. Just before the end of the century, in 1797, it was bought by Thomas Fox who came from nearby Wellington, over the county border in Somerset.

Fox was a quaker and a wool manufacturer who needed water power to expand an already flourishing business and to the existing mill he added the red brick factory which was used for the making of serge, flannel and worsted yarn for nearly two centuries until the mill was forced to close down in 1981. Now, however, new life has been breathed into the old place and once again the wool mill is open, not as a working mill but as a 'living' museum and a glimpse of how life and work in this village used to be.

Uffculme today is quite a large village, as Francis Welland, the Clerk to the Parish Council told me. "At the last census the population was just over two thousand. We've got a large variety of village shops, two village halls, three pubs, a thriving men's club, and numerous other clubs and associations. There's also a parish church, which has the longest screen in Devon and two schools, a primary and a secondary."

Two Village halls? Many parishes don't even have one. I asked Harold Norris how come? "I've explained this thousands of times to different people," he said. "The fact is that we were left about 7 or 8 acres of nice level ground by a churchman called Brice who lived in the village. It seemed only natural to develop it and put a hall there with changing rooms etc. This meant that the old church hall in Bridge Street was vacated and not used and another splinter group decided to do that up at the same time and although at the time there was a lot of dissension about it, now it appears that both halls are able to function fairly satisfactorily."

Cricket, along with the mill, has made a come back in Uffculme and although when I visited all the matches had to be played away, there were plans for the cricket club to use the field at the 'new' hall and prospects for future seasons seemed bright, especially as an artifical wicket had been put in to get the team off to a good start.

Uffculme was one of the first villages that I went to which had undertaken a Village Appraisal, a questionaire that was circulated to every adult in the village to give them a chance to express their views on village life and facilities. It covered every aspect of life in the village and district and the intention was to draw a picture of life as it is lived today as well as assessing current ammenities and facilities ranging from transport to leisure, from the church to the thorny question of having two halls in the parish.

Many villages have a variety of clubs and groups, but a mens' club was something new to me. With a membership of over 200 who come regularly for a pint and a game of cards or dominoes, the club treasurer had done his housekeeping well because just prior to my visit the club had been refurbished at a total cost of over £20,000!

Harold Norris, who had told me about Uffculme's two halls, said that a large part of the money raised for this had come from the club's one armed bandits or gaming machines. "Men don't mind if they lose a bob in them if they know it's going towards putting a new slate on the roof or to build a new billiard room."

Adrian Reed is the Chairman of the Coldharbour Mill Trust who were responsible for the re-opening of the mill and when I was there, under what was then called the Manpower Services' Commission, the Trust had over fifty people working there, many of whom came from the village and the surrounding area. "Originally the mill was only doing one process, that of spinning. Now we have modified it and if you visit you can see the whole operation from fleece off a sheep's back to spinning and then weaving."

Skating on Coldharbour Mill pond in 1914.

Thomas White was a local farmer who spoke to me on my visit and told me that there was a lot of mixed farming going on in the area around the village. "Although there's more milking herds into Uffculme than there used to be. Here" he said, "you bain't be putting this down be yer? 'cos I was about to say that there's more money in milk than in a lot of other types of farming." I did 'put it down' and it was broadcast and is probably as true today as it was then.

Thomas was nearly eighty when we met and had lived and farmed in the Culme Valley all his life. "They're a lot more affluent today than they were then. There wasn't the money about then. We used to have farm labourers who had families of about eight children or more. That's another big change. You don't get families of that size today. I suppose it was a kind of making their own 'entertainment.' They didn't go to the pub every night of the week like they do now, it was just once in a while, August Bank Holiday and things like that. But they used to have a drink mind you. They used to hang up their firkins outside the cellar door of a night-time and the farmer would fill them up and off they'd go the next day for their work. The cider was part of the wages you see. It would be nothing for fifty or sixty gallons – a hogshead – to be drunk on the farm during hay making time." No wonder they had such rosy cheeks and a merry twinkle in their eye, just like Thomas!

Doris Reynolds thinks that things have changed too. "It's not like the old days. We all made our own enjoyment then. Every street had a water pump and men would go with baths to the pumps of a Sunday night to fill them up for the women to do their washing on a Monday."

Communication is better today and Uffculme is better serviced than it used to be as Thomas White told me. "I can remember a rick fire once and I had to jump onto a pony and ride into Cullompton to tell Brooks the fireman about the fire. He had to go out into the field to catch the horses and hitch them up to the fire engine. Then on the way over to Uffculme, some six miles away, one of the horses dropped down dead! When they got there, the rick had been destroyed."

Times have changed and today, hopefully, it wouldn't take the fire engine so long. Although the working woollen mill, along with horse drawn fire engines, firkins of cider on the farm, hay ricks and waterpumps in the streets life in Uffculme is very different from how it used to be, with a population the size that the village has today I'm sure more changes are ahead for this village dominated by the tall chimney stack of Coldharbour Mill.

West Hill

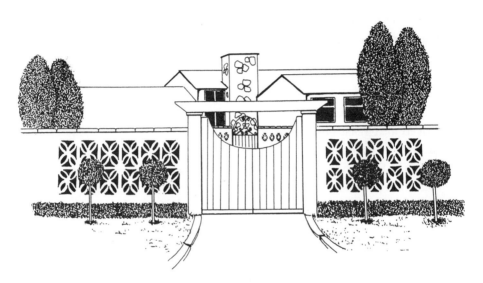

West Hill is really a suburb of the small East Devon town of Ottery St Mary, another venue in Devon for an annual tar barrel festival, but unlike Hatherleigh in the North of the County, the flaming barrels are hoisted onto the shoulder and then carried in sacking gloves through the narow streets. A frightening event which becomes more roudy as the evening wears on. Something only for the strong hearted.

My first visit to the area was when I was market gardening and during the winter I worked on a forestry nursery and sold logs as firewood. One of the people who responded to my ad in the local papers offering logs for sale, delivered to the door, was a lady from West Hill. I took the order, loaded my truck and off I set. On arrival at the house, and it's not easy to find a specific address as most of the houses are set back from the road, I met her and she closely examined the load. She then asked what type of wood it was and on explaining that it was a mixture of ash, oak and beech reluctantly said that she supposed that would do, although it had not been exactly what she was expecting. I began to unload at the edge of the driveway to the house. "Oh," she said, "couldn't you stack them in the garage, otherwise my husband will just have to move them!" I wondered quietly if her husband was disabled in some way but remembering the old addage that the 'Customer is always right' I tugged my forelock and complied with the request as she flounced off into the house without bothering to offer me a cup of tea. She did pay me however having watched me labour from behind the lace curtains.

It was perhaps the same lady who asked some friends of ours who moved into West Hill not to leave their dustbin out for too long after the refuse collectors had emptied it because it made the area look untidy! Thankfully this individual has never seen the assorted collection of bins and bags that we keep at our back door!

Although West Hill has become a suburb of Ottery and very much a dormitory for the 'professional classes' – teachers, doctors, bankers and solicitors who work in nearby Exeter – it used to be a village and have a very much more separate sense of identity than it does now. Residents still claim it as a village though and as such it must be one of the best served villages in Devon. It certainly has one of the largest village shops that I have ever seen, in the shape of Potter's Country Market, which is more like a giant supermarket than the traditional village stores. Here you can get your household needs, use the Post Office, get your hair done, buy a newspaper and even buy or sell your house!

David Price Hughes is the Residents and Rate Payers' Association Chairman and I asked him if he considered West Hill to be a village in its own right or as part of Ottery? "I think that it would be difficult to describe it as either," he said. "Until fairly recently, forty years ago or so, it was more a collection of gentlemen's houses and one or two farms. It was never really a village as such. There's no pub here, or any village green and it was the church I believe that gave its name to the place. It was called Saint Michael's on West Hill, and in a way it was a 'manufactured' community right from the very beginning."

West Hill's Post Office and Blacksmith's shop.

Potters' Country Market is run by the Potter brothers and Ken Potter told me how the business started. "The Potter family have traded on this site since 1850 when we moved here from Tipton St John. Originally it was a blacksmith's shop and that is what we did until the turn of the century. Then one member of the family went down to what is now the garage site and the Smithy went with him and this site became a dairy farm and then we had the first sub Post Office here." From this developed a taxi hire business and from the dairy farm the Potters developed a milk delivery round and then like Topsy it just grew and the building as it is today opened in 1972.

Today some eighteen hundred people live in West Hill so it's a large village and one of the residents now is a man called Frank Stensell. Frank is anything but a native of West Hill because as a German he was taken prisoner of War in the Channel Islands, moved to a P.O.W. camp at Pinhoe in Exeter before coming to work on the Potters' farm. When he came "there was still very very few houses about and it's changed completely. I couldn't believe it when I arrived, the way in which I was treated was just fantastic and people were just great to me."

Frank used to milk by hand, work with a horse to hoe the mangles and swedes and saw the farm move towards mechanisation and the village grow. When the land developed Frank took on the land that the Potters didn't need and now raises beef cattle and is the only working farmer left in the village. "I have enoyed every minute of being here. It's just wonderful."

As transport and communication improved, so the population grew and the village expanded. Their needs grew as well and in part have been met by the Potters. Socially though the village outgrew their other facilties. The school in West Hill is hoping to move to new and bigger premises and there is now a splendid new village hall at West Hill, purpose built and a lovely facility for those that live there to play short mat bowling, badminton and to join in a wide variety of activities.

From my perception of the place, perhaps the village lacks a real sense of community identity due in part I'm sure to the fact that there is no real central focus to the place physically. However there's certainly a whole range of things going on from amateur drama with the West Hill Players to the thriving groups who use the village hall described above.

It's difficult to know exactly how much further West Hill can expand, although it essentially still quite rural and spacious in feel, perhaps it has grown as large as it should but then there will I'm sure always be a demand from people wanting to come and retire or live in the village and use it as a base to commute to Exeter or ultilise the extra-ordinary facilities such as Potters Country Market or new village hall.

Whimple

The East Devon village of Whimple lies just off the busy A30 road which links Honiton to Exeter, a road that I always avoid because it is literally a death trap, although after many years of consultation there are now firm plans to re-route the road at various points which hopefully will lead to improved safety. Whimple is a place that has changed beyond all possible recognition in spirit if not physically since I first went there for the Village Profile series and in this chapter I will try and reflect some of those changes.

Earlier in this book I had recalled the days of Children's Television and Rolf Harris with his Olly the Octopus character. Before Olly there had been another children's favourite, Muffin the Mule, and his 'parents' had their home in Whimple and meeting Muffin's creators produced what I thought was a radio gem.

"We want Muffin, Muffin the Mule,
Dear Old Muffin, playing the fool,
We want Muffin, everybody sing,
We want Muffin the Mule."

Muffin the Mule with Annette Mills and Ann Hogarth.

Muffin had been one of television's first 'superstars', a wooden, black and white mule string puppet who appeared on top of a piano at which sat Annette Mills, whilst out of vision Ann Hogarth made Muffin dance to the tune she played on his strings. Ann lived in a fine Devon longhouse on the outskirts of Whimple, with her husband Jan Bussell and had one of the most extensive collections of puppets stored in their white barn 'puppet theatre' that I have ever seen. Muffin had been their baby and with Jan on his banjo, they brought him back to life for me.   Muffin was first born in 1936, although he didn't appear on television until he was ten. Annette Mills, Sir John Mills' sister, used to write the songs and act as presenter whilst Ann wrote the scripts and worked the puppet and they worked with Muffin on television every fortnight until Annette died in 1954. I asked Ann how the idea for Muffin came about. "It was Annette really, she was doing songs at the piano for the BBC and she wanted somebody to make puppets to illustrate her songs. The BBC introduced her to me and Jan and I said what about writing songs for the puppets that we've already got? So she came to our studio and picked out two or three of them, there was a clown, a puppy and Muffin and we did them in a ten minute slot. The other two didn't really get noticed, but Muffin took off from the word go." And so Muffin the Mule passed into television history and I can actually say that I have met him.

Sadly Jan Bussell died and Ann no longer lives in Whimple, but when I drive past where they used to live with Muffin and his friends I can recall the magic of a day when we went with a group of young children to a puppet show put on by Jan and Ann in the barn, which has a giant 'joker' playing card as an end window. They held the children and adults alike spell bound as they brought the puppets to life and seeing Muffin once again brought a real lump to my throat.

The demise of Muffin as a Whimple resident is not the only sad thing about the village. At one time, indeed when I visited for the Village Profile, Whimple was the base for a firm called Whiteways. Originally producing cider, the area around the village abounds in apple orchards which look glorious in flower in early summer. Latterly the firm diversified into producing British table and fortified wines. Whiteways had been a family firm which was bought out by the giant Allied Lyons Group, who as the end of the eighties grew near decided to restructure their operations. Rumours began to abound in the village that closure of the Whiteways factory with the resultant loss of hundreds of jobs was on the cards.

What was clear was that something was going on in the village because just opposite the Whiteways factory was one of the most delightful cricket grounds in the country. Inside the boundary of the field was a magnificent oak tree, which often acted as an additional fielder, and I spent a lazy summer's afternoon there enjoying, from the comfort of a deckchair, a local inter village keenly contested cricket match with a pint of beer near at hand. The perfect English summer's day, but 'storm clouds' were just over the horizon.

The firm announced that they wanted the cricket club to move from the lovely old ground, but offered recompense in the shape of a new playing field on a massive scale outside the village centre. It is now nearly completed, having been seeded last autumn. It's big, it's functional, but it's also impersonal and an entirely different kettle of fish to the intimate cricket ground that Whimple used to have. Above all it's very sad.

Not nearly as sad however as the news that Whiteways WAS to close down its Whimple based factory. When that news broke, it came as a bombshell to the village, hundreds of local people were plunged into unemployment and the factory functions were relocated. To my naïve mind, sited as it was on a rail link into Exeter, within easy striking distance of good roads and the motorway the move didn't make a lot of sense but I suppose the firm's account books and balance sheets told a different story.

Driving through the village today it is like a ghost town, inspite of a still thriving village school, scout group, shops and church Whimple will never be the same again. It is I'm sure destined for fierce planning battles in the future but is probably inexorably bound to become a commuter dormitory to Exeter. I've seen that happen in other places and personally I don't like it. But then modern times are upon us and things change, but not always for the better as I think is true in Whimple's case.

I wonder how long the lovely Whiteways Orchards around the village will survive? How long before new houses spring up on the cricket ground? How long before the factory is demolished and what has become of the people that worked there? I'm just glad that Muffin is no longer there to see it. It's enough to make a Mule cry.

Widecombe in the Moor

Mention Devon, and the West Country, and the chances are that one of the county's villages that will most readily spring to mind is the famous Widecombe in the Moor. It was Baring Gould who discovered the song which probably accounts for Widecombe's notoriety. The famous fair still takes place in September and there are those in this grey, granite village, like Simon Northmore, who would have you believe that the story of Old Uncle Tom Cobley and all is true and based on fact. What is certain is that the ghost of Cobley and the ill fated grey mare lives on in Widecombe and the villagers are certainly not anxious to disabuse anyone by telling them that it's all a made up fairy story because year after year Widecombe draws thousands of visitors all of whom are keen to hear the story retold and even sit in Tom Cobley's chair in one of the village shops!

It's not only Tom Cobley who has a place in Widecombe's folk-lore, there's another story that I was told connected with the village church, or the Cathedral of the Moor. People in the village say that everyone comes to Widecombe at some time or the other, and so perhaps it should not have been any surprise to learn that the devil had visited on one occasion. In 1638, the landlady of the Tavistock Inn at Poundsgate, near Widecombe, heard someone coming along the road. Looking out she saw a fine black horse, astride of which there was a smartly dressed gentleman. He asked her the way to Widecombe and having got directions, he then asked her for a drink. The landlady duly brought out the drink to him and in payment he threw her some coins, which she caught in her apron. Looking down she saw the coins glistening; they were made of gold. Looking back up at the horseman she heard the drink sizzling as it went down his steaming throat.

The landlady began to be afraid and hardly dared to look at the man's face and looked instead at his feet and saw to her horror that they were clad in forked boots. She had seen enough and rushed indoors, throwing the money into a pot on the bar. The man rode off and she called her husband and told him what had happened and what she had seen. To support her story she showed him the pot, which now contained nothing but dried oak leaves.

The man on the black horse, or the devil, as he was, arrived in Widecombe and at the church found the person he had come after, the warrener from Warren House Pit who had been playing a game of patience with some cards, behind one of the pillars in the church. The devil hitched his horse up to one of the pinnacles on the church tower and went inside. He grabbed the warrener by the scruff of his neck, jumped onto his horse once more and set off in the direction of Chagford, bending the pinnacle on the tower in the process. As the devil rode off, the cards fell out of his unfortunate victim's pocket and fluttered to earth. Today local people will tell you that if you go to the Warren House Inn and look back towards Widecombe, there on the moor you can pick out fields shaped like the Ace of Hearts, the Ace of Spades, Clubs and Diamonds which have remained there to this day...

Widecombe's Tom Cobley and crew.

148

The village sits in a valley and its name derives, not from a wide 'combe' but rather from Withy, the wood that abounds in the area indicating how damp the climate is – there's marshy wet lands which surround the village in which the wood thrives. The village itself is tiny with just under three hundred on the parish voting register, a small population which has dwindled over the years due to the the changes in farming methods and the loss of the manual workers on the land.

Planning restrictions in Widecombe are perhaps more strict than in other parts of the county, due to its position within the Dartmoor National Park. This means that planning consent is difficult to obtain and this in turn means that there are few openings for low cost housing leading to younger people not being able to afford to either buy or live in the village and having to move away.

On my first visit to the village it was a delight to meet Canon Hall, who was then in his nineties. He told of the tremendous changes that he had seen in village life, of the times when the hearths in the cottages burned peat, which never went out stacked around and on the concave top of the cooking pot, with a bit of rabbit or bacon in, so making a perfect oven. He also told me a story of how Latin came to be spoken in the parish for the first time for hundreds of years. There was an old lady in the village who had a gift of healing what they used to call the King's Evil, or skin disease. "She had a knowledge of herbs and went down to the brook to collect them. She then made up a confection, or what we'd call an embrocation and people came from all over the place to be cured. What she did was to take this embrocation and gently massage it into the hand and wrap it in a bit of wool or linen, and say come again in a month and it was alright."

"Well I went to her one day and I said to her, Granny do tell me how you do it? What happens? She said, you want the milk of a red cow, the wool of a black sheep and a sprig of hawthorn, but it doesn't really matter about the hawthorn my dear. Then you make it up into an embrocation. And then what do you do? I asked. Oh then she says, I stikes 'em. I couldn't make head nor tail of that but then being a parson I remembered my bible and that strike is the old word 'stroke'. So, then I said, what do you do? Oh, she said I make the sign of the cross and then I say In nomni domni. I realised that she was really saying In nomine domine. She was speaking Latin which they hadn't heard in this parish for five hundred years!"

Whichever of the Widecombe stories you choose to believe Canon Hall's remains one of my favourites. Although it's easy to imagine the rattling of bones of Tom Pearce's ghostly grey mare down Widecombe Hill, or relish the story of the card player who was taken off by the devil, Canon Hall's obvious pleasure in telling of the rediscovery of Latin as a spoken language in this famous Dartmoor village holds a warm place in my memory – as warm of those pots bubbling under the glowing peat in what he described as "the wonderful old days".

Winkleigh

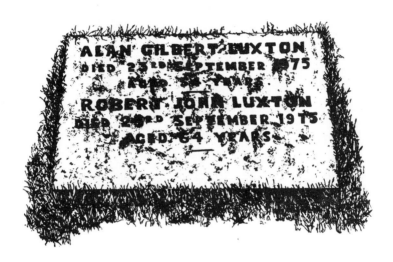

Although I had heard of Winkleigh in mid Devon, it wasn't until quite late on in the series that I actually visited the village, initially led there by way of a book which had been published following the deaths of the last surviving members of a Devon farming family who had worked West Chapple farm, just outside the village, for generations.

At the time the newspaper headlines were full of reports of the second assassination attempt on the life of Gerald Ford, then President of the U.S.A., and of the Spaghetti House Siege in London, but in late September of 1975, the media's attention switched to the story of the Luxtons of Winkleigh.

Jimmy Reynolds, who worked in a butcher's shop in nearby Hatherleigh, was delivering meat to the farm and having parked his van, he was walking towards the farmhouse when he saw what at first he took to be a crumpled scarecrow laying in the cobbled yard in front of the house.

West Chapple Farm today.

"I decided to have a look at this scarecrow thing to see what it was and it turned out to be a body in a rather nasty state."

The 'scarecrow' was in fact the body of Alan Luxton who with his older brother Robbie and their sister Francis had lived at West Chapple Farm all their lives. Jimmy Reynolds called the Police and the investigation into what happened was headed by the then Head of the Devon and Cornwall Constabulary C.I.D., Proven Sharpe.

When I first met Proven, he arrived at the Radio Devon studios clutching a Tesco's carrier bag, inside of which he carried the Police file on the Luxtons' case. I will never ever forget the scene of crime photographs that he showed me and the then Programme Organiser, Mike Gibbons.

The two brothers and their sister had died of horrific shot gun wounds at fairly close range, and it was this story that was splashed over the front pages the following day, although at that stage was had happened remained a mystery.

Proven Sharpe told me "When I arrived three bodies had been discovered. There was one in front of the farmhouse and the bodies of Robert and his sister were in the garden at the rear. Clearly it was a murder inquiry because quite obviously from the circumstances one person had not died as a result of self inflicted wounds."

In the programme which I prepared on the Luxton case, I once again used the 'vox pop' as a device to try and paint a picture of the Luxtons as remembered by their neighbours and the people of Winkleigh. "We first heard of their deaths on the television news that evening. As soon as they said that the bodies of two men and their sister had been found on a North Devon farm, I'm afraid that I rather knew which farm it was. I realised when they said the name of the farm that morning when I was getting my cows in I had heard a shotgun fired which I had imagined was the Luxtons shooting a fox. I wish to God it were... It was a terrible shock to the whole village. Winkleigh was shattered... Everybody sort of respected them and no-one thought that they would do a thing like that... "Like what? What exactly had happened at West Chapple? That was the puzzle that faced Proven Sharpe and the Police in their investigation.

Proven Sharpe.

"In the early stages one has always got to keep an open mind in any criminal investigation," Proven Sharpe told me "and mustn't rush to any immediate conclusions and whilst it appeared that it was a matter of an internal incident in which no fourth person or other person was involved we couldn't at that stage eliminate that possibility."

The Home Office Pathologist was called in along with forensic scientists to try and piece together what had happened and enquiries were made to try and establish what sort of people the Luxtons had been. Jimmy Reynolds told me that "I didn't really know them very well. I don't think that anybody really knew them."

Gradually the pieces of the jigsaw were fitted together. Having worked the farm for generations Robbie, the older brother felt that things were getting too much to manage as old age came on and he and his sister, Frances, had decided to sell up and move. Alan, the younger brother was opposed to the move and without any offspring to pass the farm onto, Alan was 'outvoted.' But the prospect of selling was a matter of great anguish to all three and they had great diffiulty in coming to terms with having to leave West Chapple behind them. As a neighbour told me, "This was the biggest decision that they had ever had to make in their lives. Whether to carry on with the farm which had become phsyically too much of burden at the age of sixty or so, or to sell, that was what created the tension. "Another neighbour recalled that "Alan said he never intended to leave the farm and I think it got him down and he shot himself first, and Robbie, well he was so shocked that he did his sister first and then did himself afterwards."

Proven Sharpe said "Initially it did look like one brother had shot the other one and then his sister, but this is where you get the value of the forensic experts and the pathologist because ultimately it didn't turn out that way at all. When Alan's body was found there was no weapon beside the body and it was only as a result of a fairly detailed examination of the scene that it became clear that he had shot himself. When we examined the scene, it had been obvious from the outset that next to the body there was a pronged stick which is a common implement to be found beside the body of someone who has shot themselves with a shot gun. Then in the hard soil next to the body in the farmyard we found the indentation of the base of the butt of a shot gun. This clearly indicated that the gun had been held perpendicular, with the butt down on the ground, that Alan had seized hold of the barrel and then activated the trigger by means of the short pronged stick."

"It then became fairly clear that Robert had found his brother dead in front of the house, seized hold of the gun and shot his sister in the back garden and then turned the gun on himself because again there was the presence of a stick beside his body."

There was much speculation about the family, reports that they were somehow eccentric recluses who hardly ever left the farm. Some thought that they had no mains water or electricity, although they had both, and that their farming methods had changed little over the years and that they still worked the farm by hand with no modern farming aids. A photographer friend who went to West Chapple however clearly remembers a tractor parked in one of the barns, something which was confirmed by a former rector of Winkleigh, although he does recall that the under side of the rear mudguards were lined with silver foil to protect the wheel arches from mud being sprayed up from the wheels, a sign of how careful they were. I have since heard of a local builder who installed a new bathroom for them and had to account for every last screw used.

Proven Sharpe was able to refute the story of the Luxtons being recluses – "They were seen about in the village and did to a certain extent take part in village life, although for some months before their deaths they had disassociated themselves with much activity in the village and had become pretty well withdrawn and introverted." A measure perhaps of how heavily the decision on whether to sell what after all was the family heritage or not must have weighed on them.

As Proven said "It was a sad end to people who had lived their lives on that farm but at the end of the day couldn't cope with the realities of the situation and sadly they just destroyed themselves."

The story of the Luxtons haunted me for a long time and in spite of several months of work, visiting the farm, meeting and recording interviews with people who had known them, I felt at the end of the day I really knew very little about them. I have no idea for instance what they looked like, in spite of having seen the Police file photographs. An intriguing and as Proven Sharpe had said a very sad end to a family who had been in Winkleigh since the fourteenth century. Writing this, the story floods back in all its poignancy to haunt me again and I don't think that anyone will really know what happened or what went on in the minds of the Luxtons on that fateful day in September 1975, when they met their deaths.

Frances Luxton's grave at Brushford Barton.

Acknowledgements

All original line drawings by **ROBIN MURRAY.**

Grateful thanks to the following:

Jeff Skinner for his editing skills, Laurence Daeche of the Anonymous Design Company for his design and Brian Eveleigh for his studio work on the photographs contained in this book which have been reproduced by kind permission of the copyright owners, who reserve all rights. Typesetting by P&M Typesetting Ltd, Exeter. Printed by Greenaways, Stroud.

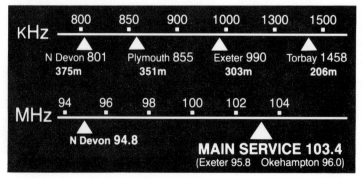

_ᴑᴨ_

Front cover – Sheila Ellis – The Clovelly Collection.
The Search for Genette Tate – The Devon and Cornwall Constabulary.
Paul Simon – Alan Kleinberg courtesy of WEA Records.
Nigel Fitzhugh – Radio Times.
Branscombe's Bakers – Stewart Collier courtesy of the National Trust.
Braunton Great Field – Braunton Museum.
Broadhembury – Mrs Rex Lawrence.
Broadwoodwidger – South West Water Authority.
Chagford – Chris Smith.
Clovelly – Sheila Ellis – The Clovelly Collection.
Drewsteignton – Jack Price.
Gittisham – Clive Essame.
Hatherleigh from the air – Dennis Bater.
Hemyock – Brian Clist.
Luppitt – Patrick Woodroffe; Buddhist Monk – Lyn Baker.
Lydford – Chris Smith.
Lynmouth – Courtesy E.R. Delderfield from his book 'The Lynmouth Flood Disaster.'
Moretonhampstead – The Dartmoor National Park.
Musbury – Musbury Post Office.
Newton Ferrers – The Newton Ferrers Regatta Committee.
Otterton – Desna Greenhow, Otterton Mill.
Payhembury – Louise Granger.
Princetown – Cell Interior – John Lyne; Prison exterior – Brian Eveleigh.
Spreyton – Chris Smith.
Swimbridge – North Devon Athenaeum.
Tetcott – Maurice Thomas of the South Tetcott Hunt.
Uffculme – Cold Harbour Mill.
West Hill – Ken Potter.
Whimple – BBC Television.
Widecombe – Chris Smith.
Winkleigh – Chris Smith, The Express & Echo & Chris Smith.
Back Cover – Mike Alsford for Radio Times.